"Mission statement work is the single most important work because the decisions made there affect all other decisions."

—Dr. Stephen Covey
author of *The 7 Habits of Highly Successful People*

101
MISSION
STATEMENTS
FROM TOP COMPANIES

PLUS GUIDELINES FOR WRITING
YOUR OWN MISSION STATEMENT

JEFFREY ABRAHAMS

TEN SPEED PRESS
Berkeley | Toronto

The inclusion of these mission statements is not intended to convey business information to be relied upon in generating business statements or in making business decisions. The publisher does not explicitly or implicitly offer any representation or warranty that these mission statements will be of any use in forming a business conclusion.

Each mission statement is reprinted exactly as it was received from the company of origin.

Ten Speed Press
PO Box 7123
Berkeley CA 94707
www.tenspeed.com

Distributed in Australia by Simon and Schuster Australia, in Canada by Ten Speed Press Canada, in New Zealand by Southern Publishers Group, in South Africa by Real Books, and in the United Kingdom and Europe by Publishers Group UK.

Cover and interior design by Laura Milton

Library of Congress Cataloging-in-Publication Data
Abrahams, Jeffrey.
 101 mission statements from top companies / Jeffrey Abrahams.
    p. cm.
 ISBN-10: 1-58008-761-2 (alk. paper)
 ISBN-13: 978-1-58008-761-2 (alk. paper)
 1. Mission statements--Authorship. 2. Mission statements--United States. I. Title. II. Title: One hundred and one mission statements from top companies.
  HD30.285.A267 1999
  658.4'012--dc22

                    2006037617

ISBN 13: 978-1-58091-761-2
ISBN 10: 1-58091-761-2

First printing, 2007
Printed in the United States of America
1 2 3 4 5 6 7 8 9 10 / 09 08 07

ACKNOWLEDGMENTS

It took more than two years of research and release-form wrangling to complete this book. Thus, I am very grateful to representatives from each of the companies profiled for granting me written permission to reprint the text of their proprietary mission and vision statements.

My personal mission to get this information into your hands, dear reader, would not have been accomplished without the support of the mission-savvy people at Ten Speed Press. To Lorena Jones, publisher, thanks for sticking with this project and believing in the merit of the subject as well as the author. And to my editor Veronica Randall, abundant huzzahs to you for doggedly unsnarling all the knotty issues this project presented to you. Thanks are also due to Laura Milton for a fresh, sleek design. Finally, thanks to Phil Wood for welcoming me into the family of Ten Speed Press authors so long ago and keeping the door open to receive my ideas and proposals for projects.

TABLE OF CONTENTS

PART 01:
HOW TO USE THIS RESOURCE

PART 02:
THE COMPANIES
AND THEIR STATEMENTS

TABLE OF CONTENTS (CONTINUED)

TABLE OF CONTENTS (CONTINUED)

PART 01: HOW TO USE THIS RESOURCE

This book has been designed to help you understand the nature, structure, style, and language of a company positioning statement known generally as a mission statement. It is also intended to provide a how-to guide to help you write or rewrite your organization's statement, whether you work for a large corporation, small company, a nonprofit organization, government agency, municipality, or university.

Part 01 offers some guidelines for writing a mission, vision, or other type of company statement. Part 02 is a compendium of 101 mission statements selected from the *Fortune* 1000 and other sources.

As you know, writing can be hard work. And when something as important and visible as a mission statement is being created, there may be many editors who have a hand at shaping the final words. Therefore, the guidelines I have provided are intended to help *facilitate* the process, not automatically formulate the results.

COMPANIES ARE LIKE PEOPLE — THEY NEED A MISSION

Whenever and wherever men and women have endeavored to achieve something purposefully, a statement of mission or purpose is pronounced. It precedes the first step in a long march. And it is etched in stone over the entrances of great buildings. People, by their very nature, seem to ennoble a task by endowing it with a stated mission.

Corporations as entities and people as individuals share certain characteristics. Over time, they develop personalities that shape their philosophies and motivate their actions. And without a purpose or a mission, both a person and a company will flounder.

Shaping the identity of a corporation really begins with defining its mission. Its reason for being. Its purpose. Focus. Goal.

Every company, no matter how big or small, needs a mission statement as a source of direction, a kind of compass, that lets its employees, its customers, and even its stockholders know what it stands for and where it's headed.

A mission engenders a company with a sense of purposefulness by asserting the reason for its existence.

A mission also serves to unify people in a company, especially when it is comprised of many different kinds of people, in different parts of the country and the world, with varying job titles as well as different levels of training and education. As a unifying touchstone, a mission provides the company and its employees with a sense of identity.

And finally, a mission, simply by its very existence, provides a foundation on which the company can build its future.

A BLUEPRINT
FOR SUCCESS

There's another way of perceiving what a mission is all about. Consider a mission as part of the set of fundamental principles by which a business operates. The rest of the set could include a vision, goal, slate of operating principles, ethics statement, an environmental policy, and a basic business philosophy—among many other statements.

Thinking of a mission statement as part of a company's overall blueprint for success—and communicating that to employees, customers and the public—gives a company a head start on achieving that success.

Please note: I use the term "mission statement" to include a broad range of approaches and titles used by a wide variety of companies. Some companies put their vision and/or values statements before their mission, if they have one. Simply by shaping a "statement," these companies are stating or implying their corporate mission.

TARGET AUDIENCE—
THIS MISSION'S FOR YOU

For whom is a mission statement intended? Is it meant for the employees of a company? The members of an organization? The general public? Present or future vendors or clients? In truth, there is no wrong answer to this question. In fact, some companies compose their mission statement in a way that is intended to address all possible audiences. Others purposely create a mission statement that is strictly intended for in-house use only. Still others post their mission in their annual reports, which are made available to prospective investors as well as current shareholders.

In some cases, the target audience is specifically mentioned and therefore clearly identified in the mission statement itself. In instances when more than one audience can be identified, multiple audiences can be addressed within the statement. It is not uncommon for a single mission statement to contain:

To our staff . . .

To our employees . . .

To our customers . . .

To our clients . . .

To our colleagues . . .

To our partners . . .

To our stockholders . . .

To our patrons . . .

To our community . . .

The target audience, or audiences, will have a significant impact on the length, tone, and visibility of the mission statement. However, an emphasis on collective goals, acknowledgment of achievements, dedication to values, and commitment to service are the universal ideals that are most commonly expressed.

LENGTH: HOW LONG IS LONG ENOUGH?

According to a popular folk legend, when Abraham Lincoln was president, he was asked by a reporter, "How long should a man's legs be?" Lincoln is said to have responded, "Long enough to reach the ground."

The same is true for a mission statement.

For some companies, a single sentence is sufficient. Others have produced great, lengthy documents that begin with a mission and include vision statements, values, philosophies, objectives, plans and strategies in supporting roles. And still others are somewhere in between, longer than one line, but contained within one page.

All that's necessary is that the mission be long enough to reach the target audience.

KEY WORDS

Key words and phrases also set the tone for a statement. The following is a list of key words that have appeared in mission statements I have examined over the last sixteen years of research:

Ability	Diversity	Joy	Return
Accomplished	Employees	Leader	on equity
Accountable	Empower	Leadership	Revolutionize
Alignment	Enrich	Life	Risk
Asset	Enthusiasm	Long-term	Satisfy
Best	Ethics	Loyalty	Security
Brand	Exceeding	Marketplace	Serve
Change	Excellence	Mission	Service
Citizens	Exciting	Mutual	Shared
Commitment	Expertise	Neighbor	Shareholders
Communicate	Extraordinary	Obligation	Solution
Communities	Fair	Opportunities	Spirit
Connect	Flexibility	Passion	Strategy
Conscience	Fun	Performance	Strength
Cooperation	Future	Positive	Success
Corporate	Goal	Potential	Support
citizen	Goodwill	Power	Talented
Creativity	Growth	Pride	Team
Critical	Harmony	Principles	Teamwork
Culture	Heritage	Productivity	Together
Customers	Icon	Profit	Tomorrow
Dedicated	Ideas	Prosperity	Trust
Dedication	Individual	Quality	Unique
Difference	Information	Relationships	Unity
Dignity	Initiative	Reliable	Values
Direct	Innovation	Respect	Vision
Disciplined	Integrity	Responsibility	Win

A STEP-BY-STEP GUIDE TO WRITING A MISSION STATEMENT

STEP 1:
DECIDE WHO IS GOING TO WRITE THE MISSION STATEMENT.
Is this a solo task or a group effort? Take a lesson from the real-life examples of other companies and consider the advantages of creating a committee with representatives from every department in your company. That way, everyone will have a chance to feel like they had a voice in the statement's creation and will be more likely to embrace its content and spirit.

STEP 2:
AGREE ON WHEN THE STATEMENT IS GOING TO BE WRITTEN.
During business hours or in evening sessions? In a single weekend? At the office or off-site where there will be fewer distractions? And how much time will you allow? A single afternoon or evening? A weekend? A month? Six-months? A year? Impose a deadline and stick to it.

STEP 3:
DETERMINE THE TARGET AUDIENCE(S).
Employees of your company? Customers? Suppliers? Stockholders? The general public? You have to figure out **who** you're talking to before you can figure out **what** to say.

STEP 4:
DECIDE WHAT KIND OF LANGUAGE IS APPROPRIATE.
Start with a list of key words and phrases that apply to your business. Bring a group of people together, roll out an easel, invite a free flow of ideas, and write down words and phrases that come to mind. Refer to the list of key words provided earlier.

This may lead to a discussion about what kind of statement you're writing in the first place and what its title should be. You may wish to create a mission statement that describes your company's purpose or goals. But you may also want to include a strategy statement that outlines how your company is going to achieve its goals. And that's only the beginning. Remember, there are values statements, statements of principles, philosophies, environmental policies, and more. Ultimately, it's up to you to decide the nature, length, and tone of the document.

STEP 5: ADOPT A FORMAT.

Will the mission statement be presented to the target audience in the annual report? Will it be beautifully printed on quality paper, designed for framing and distribution? Will it appear in a brochure or pamphlet and made available to the public? Will it be incorporated into corporate gift items, such as a wallet-sized, laminated card? Embedded in a Lucite paperweight? Printed on a company calendar or coffee mug? Silk-screened onto a T-shirt or sweatshirt? Emblazoned on a banner? Engraved in granite? Or displayed on a brass plaque on the front door?

If you are proud of your mission statement, you will want to communicate its message in a variety of ways that reflect your company's distinctive brand and culture.

PART 02:
THE COMPANIES
AND THEIR
STATEMENTS

In this section, you'll find profiles of 101 companies representing a wide variety of industries. I am providing these as examples to inspire you and provide some guidance for creating your own mission statement or statement of vision, values, aspirations, purpose, creed, strategy or philosophy.

The limited space of this book's format necessitated that, in some cases, I include only one or two of an individual company's positioning statements. For the whole story, please refer to each company's website listed in the address portion of each company profile.

Please note: No attempt has been made to analyze or criticize the content of the company statements. That is not the purpose of this book. Instead, I am presenting the following as interesting examples worthy of your attention.

3M COMPANY

OUR VALUES
· Provide investors an attractive return through sustained, quality growth.
· Satisfy customers with superior quality, value, and service.
· Respect our social and physical environment.
· Be a company employees are proud to be part of.

CORPORATE DESCRIPTION
3M (NYSE: MMM) is a diversified technology company with a world-wide presence in the following markets: consumer and office; display and graphics; electronics and communications; health care; industrial; safety, security and protective services; and transportation.

ADDRESS
3M Center
St. Paul, MN 55144
www.3m.com

ADOBE SYSTEMS INCORPORATED

MISSION STATEMENT

Adobe revolutionizes how the world engages with ideas and information.

CORPORATE DESCRIPTION

For more than two decades, Adobe software and technologies have redefined business, entertainment, and personal communications by setting new standards for producing and delivering content that engages people virtually anywhere at anytime. From rich images in print, video, and film to dynamic digital content for a variety of media, the impact of Adobe solutions is felt by anyone who creates, views, and interacts with information. With a portfolio of many of the most respected and recognizable software brands, Adobe is one of the world's largest and most diversified software companies.

ADDRESS

345 Park Avenue
San Jose, CA 95110
www.adobe.com

ALBERTO-CULVER COMPANY

THE ALBERTO-CULVER MISSION

The Alberto-Culver Company is dedicated to building, for the long-term, profitable businesses and substantial brands which are recognized for bringing innovation and value to consumers and an excellent return to shareholders. These goals can best be achieved by:

Fostering the entrepreneurial spirit, flexibility, and marketing innovation which have helped build the company through the fulfillment of identified consumer needs.

Instilling in all employees the recognition that they are each business builders, and providing a framework that acknowledges the worth of the individual while promoting development of the teamwork which is critical to our success.

Recognizing the need for responsive customer service systems and working to ensure that a superior level of service is available to the customers we sell and from the vendors we choose.

Deploying all our resources in a manner that minimizes product development time from idea to marketplace.

Pursuing and maximizing opportunities to grow our business, focusing on areas of our expertise and trade strengths, wherever those opportunities may originate.

CORPORATE DESCRIPTION

Alberto-Culver Company is a global manufacturer and marketer of beauty, personal care, and household products sold under leading brand names such as Alberto VO5, Nexxus, TRESemme, St. Ives, Motions, Soft & Beautiful, Just For Me, Mrs. Dash, and Static Guard.

ADDRESS

2525 Armitage Avenue
Melrose Park, IL 60160
www.alberto.com

ALCOA

VISION STATEMENT

At Alcoa, our vision is to be the best company in the world.

Note: Please see the company's website for its extensive statement of company values that support the Vision Statement.

CORPORATE DESCRIPTION

Alcoa is the world's leading producer and manager of primary aluminum, fabricated aluminum and alumina facilities, and is active in all major aspects of the industry. Alcoa serves the aerospace, automotive, packaging, building and construction, commercial transportation and industrial markets, bringing design, engineering, production and other capabilities of Alcoa's businesses to customers.

ADDRESS

201 Isabella Street
Pittsburgh, PA 15212
www.alcoa.com

AMERICAN EXPRESS COMPANY

AMERICAN EXPRESS COMPANY VALUES

Customer Commitment: We develop relationships that make a positive difference in our customers' lives.

Quality: We provide outstanding products and unsurpassed service that, together, deliver premium value to our customers.

Integrity: We uphold the highest standards of integrity in all of our actions.

Teamwork: We work together, across boundaries, to meet the needs of our customers and to help the company win.

Respect for People: We value our people, encourage their development, and reward their performance.

Good Citizenship: We are good citizens in the communities in which we live and work.

A Will to Win: We exhibit a strong will to win in the marketplace and in every aspect of our business.

Personal Accountability: We are personally accountable for delivering on our commitments.

The Result: To the extent we act according to these values, we believe we will inspire the loyalty of our customers, earn a sustainable leadership position in our business, attract and retain a highly talented and engaged workforce, and provide a superior return to our shareholders. This, in turn, will enable us to achieve our vision of becoming the world's most respected service brand.

AMERICAN EXPRESS COMPANY (CONTINUED)

CORPORATE DESCRIPTION
American Express Company is a diversified worldwide travel, financial and network services company founded in 1850. It is a leader in charge and credit cards, Travelers Cheques, travel, business services, insurance, and international banking.

ADDRESS
World Financial Center
200 Vesey Street
New York, NY 10285
www.americanexpress.com

AMERICAN FAMILY INSURANCE GROUP

MISSION STATEMENT

American Family's mission is to provide financial protection to an expanding customer base with a commitment to best value.

CORPORATE DESCRIPTION

American Family Insurance Group is a multi-line insurance provider with a wide variety of products for individuals, families, and businesses. It offers financial services and property, auto, commercial, health, and life insurance in eighteen states.

ADDRESS

6000 American Parkway
Madison, WI 53783
www.americanfamilyinsurance.com

AMGEN INC.

OUR MISSION
To serve patients

OUR ASPIRATION
We aspire to be the best human therapeutics company. We will live the Amgen values and use science and innovation to dramatically improve people's lives.

OUR VALUES
- Be Science-Based
- Compete Intensely and Win
- Create Value for Patients, Staff and Stockholders
- Be Ethical
- Trust and Respect Each Other
- Ensure Quality
- Work in Teams
- Collaborate, Communicate and Be Accountable

CORPORATE DESCRIPTION
Amgen is a leading therapeutics company in the biotechnology industry.

ADDRESS
One Amgen Center Drive
Thousand Oaks, CA 91320
www.amgen.com

ANHEUSER-BUSCH COMPANIES, INC.

OUR VISION
Through all our products, services and relationships, we will add to life's enjoyment.

OUR MISSION
- Be the world's beer company
- Enrich and entertain a global audience
- Deliver superior returns to our shareholders

OUR VALUES
- Quality in everything we do
- Exceeding customer expectations
- Trust, respect and integrity in all of our relationships
- Continuous improvement, innovation and embracing change
- Teamwork and open, honest communication
- Each employee's responsibility for contributing to the company's success
- Creating a safe, productive and rewarding work environment
- Building a high-performing, diverse workforce
- Promoting the responsible consumption of our products
- Preserving and protecting the environment and supporting communities where we do business

CORPORATE DESCRIPTION
Based in St. Louis, Missouri, Anheuser-Busch, Cos., Inc. is the leading American brewer holding 50 percent of the U.S. beer market. The company is American-owned and brews the world's largest-selling beers, Budweiser and Bud Light. Anheuser-Busch also holds a 50 percent share in Grupo Modelo, Mexico's leading brewer, and a 27 percent share in Tsingtao, the number one brewer in China. Anheuser-Busch is ranked

ANHEUSER-BUSCH
COMPANIES, INC. (CONTINUED)

first in the U.S. beverage industry in *Fortune* magazine's 2005 "America's Most Admired Companies" and in the top thirty on *Fortune's* 2005 "Global Most Admired Companies" list. The company is one of the largest theme park operators in the United States, is a major manufacturer of aluminum cans, and is the world's largest recycler of aluminum beverage containers.

ADDRESS
One Busch Place
St. Louis, MO 63118
www.anheuser-busch.com

APPLIED MATERIALS, INC.

OUR MISSION

To be the global leader in nanomanufacturing technology solutions for the electronics industry, through differentiated and innovative system, service, and software products, providing our customers a trusted path to superior results.

OUR VISION

We apply nanomanufacturing technology to improve the way people live.

CORPORATE DESCRIPTION

Applied Materials, Inc. (NASDAQ: AMAT) is the global leader in nano-manufacturing technology™ solutions for the electronics industry with a broad portfolio of innovative equipment, service and software products.

ADDRESS

3050 Bowers Avenue
P.O. Box 58039
Santa Clara, CA 95054
www.appliedmaterials.com

AQUILA, INC.

VISION

To provide energy for better living.

MISSION

To exceed expectations in providing safe and reliable electric and natural gas services.

Note: Please refer to the company's website to see its statement of Critical Success Factors and Values.

CORPORATE DESCRIPTION

Based in Kansas City, Missouri, Aquila, Inc. (NYSE: ILA) operates electricity and natural gas distribution utilities serving customers in seven U.S. states. Aquila also owns and operates power generation assets.

ADDRESS

20 West Ninth Street
Kansas City, MO 64105
www.aquila.com

ARAMARK

OUR BUSINESS PURPOSE

· We are a **professional services** organization dedicated to excellence.

· We develop and sustain our leadership position by engaging and supporting our most valuable and differentiated asset; the competence, commitment and creativity of **our people.**

· We provide world-class **experiences, environments, and outcomes** for our clients and customers by developing relationships based on service excellence, partnership and mutual understanding.

· We enable our clients to realize their **core mission,** and we will anticipate the needs and exceed the expectations of customers, by dedicating our skills in professional services—hospitality, food, facilities and uniforms—to the goals and priorities of their institution.

· We create **long-term value** and capture the greatest opportunity for all ARAMARK stakeholders—our people, clients, customers, communities and shareholders—by delivering sustainable, **profitable growth** in sales, earnings and cash flow in a **global company** built on pride, integrity and respect.

CORPORATE DESCRIPTION

ARAMARK (NYSE: RMK) is a leader in professional services, providing award-winning food services, facilities management, and uniform and career apparel to health care institutions, universities and school districts, stadiums and arenas, and businesses around the world.

In *Fortune* magazine's 2006 list of "America's Most Admired Companies," ARAMARK was ranked number one in its industry, and, since 1998, has consistently ranked one of the top three most admired companies in its industry as evaluated by peers and industry analysts. The

ARAMARK (CONTINUED)

company was also ranked first in its industry in the 2005 *Fortune* 500 survey. ARAMARK has approximately 240,000 employees serving clients in nineteen countries.

ADDRESS
1101 Market Street
Philadelphia, PA 19107
www.aramark.com

ARMSTRONG WORLD INDUSTRIES, INC.

MISSION
Simpler
Faster
Better...
Together

VISION
We deliver on our promises

Values
Respect
Integrity
Diversity
Service

Note: An Armstrong representative indicated that the company's vision, mission, and values are presented on banners that are displayed in all of Armstrong's buildings on the Lancaster Campus and in all plants and offices worldwide. For international use, the banners have been translated into seven languages including Italian, French, Spanish, Dutch, German, Swedish, and Chinese.

CORPORATE DESCRIPTION
Armstrong Holdings, Inc., is the parent company of Armstrong World Industries, Inc., a global leader in the design and manufacture of floors, ceilings and cabinets. Based in Lancaster, Pennsylvania, Armstrong operates forty-one plants in twelve countries and has approximately 14,900 employees worldwide.

ARMSTRONG WORLD INDUSTRIES, INC. (CONTINUED)

ADDRESS
2500 Columbia Avenue
Lancaster, PA 17604
www.armstrong.com

BECTON, DICKINSON AND COMPANY

VALUES

Purpose
We help all people live healthy lives.

Goal
Become the organization most known for eliminating unnecessary suffering and death from disease, and in so doing, become one of the best performing companies in the world.

Core Values
We treat each other with respect. BD associates act with respect toward each other and toward those with whom we interact. We disagree openly and honestly, and we deal with our differences professionally. Once we have made a decision, we act together in harmony.

We do what is right. We are committed to the highest standards of excellence in everything that we do: on behalf of our customers, our shareholders, our communities, and ourselves. We are proud to work for a health care company whose products and services make a difference in people's lives. We derive our greatest sense of accomplishment from doing what is right—not what is expedient. We are reliable, honest, and trustworthy in all our dealings. We keep our promises and if we make a mistake we put it right.

We always seek to improve. Superior quality is the "ground floor" of our organization. Upon it we continually strive to improve by developing, manufacturing and supplying products and services superior to our competitors' and better than the previous one. We study our progress and learn from ourselves and others how to do things more effectively

BECTON, DICKINSON
AND COMPANY (CONTINUED)

and efficiently. Our commitment to quality goes beyond how well we serve our customers to include the way we deal with all people. How we do things is as important to us as what we do.

We accept personal responsibility. We consider individual involvement and accountability to be both a right and a privilege and accept personal responsibility for everything that we do. We treat the company's reputation as our own and try to make wise use of our time and the company's resources. We expect access to the tools and information necessary to participate in any decisions that will reflect on our collective or individual reputations.

CORPORATE DESCRIPTION

Becton, Dickinson and Company is a medical technology company that serves health care institutions, life science researchers, clinical laboratories, industry, and the general public. Organized by three segments: BD Biosciences, BD Diagnostics, and BD Medical, BD manufactures and sells a broad range of medical supplies, devices, laboratory equipment and diagnostic products.

Note: This text is provided courtesy of Becton, Dickinson and Company.

ADDRESS
1 Becton Drive
Franklin Lakes, NJ 07417
www.bd.com

BEN & JERRY'S HOMEMADE, INC.

OUR MISSION STATEMENT
Ben & Jerry's is founded on and dedicated to a sustainable corporate concept of linked prosperity.

Our mission consists of three interrelated parts:

Product Mission: To make, distribute and sell the finest quality all natural ice cream and euphoric concoctions with a continued commitment to incorporating wholesome, natural ingredients and promoting business practices that respect the Earth and the Environment.

Economic Mission: To operate the company on a sustainable financial basis of profitable growth, increasing value for our stakeholders and expanding opportunities for development and career growth for our employees.

Social Mission: To operate the company in a way that actively recognizes the central role that business plays in society by initiating innovative ways to improve the quality of life locally, nationally, and internationally.

Central to the Mission of Ben & Jerry's: Is the belief that all three parts must thrive equally in a manner that commands deep respect for individuals within and outside the company and supports the communities of which they are a part.

CORPORATE DESCRIPTION
Ben & Jerry's produces a wide variety of super-premium ice cream and ice cream novelties, using dairy products from a Vermont dairy cooperative and high-quality ingredients. The company is committed to using

BEN & JERRY'S
HOMEMADE, INC. (CONTINUED)

milk and cream from cows that have not been treated with the synthetic hormone rBGH, and states its position on rBGH on its labels. Ben and Jerry's products are distributed nationwide and in selected foreign countries in supermarkets, grocery stores, convenience stores, franchise Ben & Jerry's Scoop Shops, restaurants and other venues.

ADDRESS
30 Community Drive
South Burlington, VT 05403
www.benjerry.com

BNSF RAILWAY COMPANY (BURLINGTON NORTHERN AND SANTA FE RAILWAY COMPANY)

VISION & VALUES

Delivering What's Important: Our vision is to realize the tremendous potential of BNSF Railway by providing transportation services that consistently meet our customers' expectations. A vision statement is only as good as the people who work to bring it to life each day. To live the vision, the diverse group of more than 38,000 professionals who comprise the BNSF community embrace a set of shared values:

- Listening to customers and doing what it takes to meet their expectations
- Empowering one another, showing concern for our colleagues' well-being, and respect for their talents and achievements
- Continuously improving by striving to do the right thing safely and efficiently
- Celebrating our rich heritage and building on our success as we shape our promising future

CORPORATE DESCRIPTION

A subsidiary of Burlington Northern Santa Fe Corporation (NYSE: BNI), BNSF Railway Company operates one of the largest railroad networks in North America, with about 32,000 route miles in twenty-eight states and two Canadian provinces.

ADDRESS

2650 Lou Menk Drive
Fort Worth, TX 76131
www.bnsf.com

BORGWARNER INC.

OUR VISION

BorgWarner is the recognized leader in advanced products and technologies that satisfy customer needs in powertrain components and systems solutions.

WHAT WE VALUE: THE BORGWARNER BELIEFS

Respect for each other. BorgWarner must operate in a climate of openness, trust, and cooperation, in which each of us freely grants others the same respect and decency we seek for ourselves. We expect open, honest, and timely communication. As a global company, we invite and embrace the diversity of all our people.

Power of collaboration. BorgWarner is both a community of entrepreneurial businesses and a single enterprise. Our goal is to preserve the freedom each of us needs to find personal satisfaction while building a strong business that comes from unity of purpose. True unity is more than a melding of self-interests; it results when goals and values are shared.

Passion for excellence. BorgWarner chooses to be a leader—in serving our customers, advancing our technologies, and rewarding all who invest in us. To sustain our leadership, we relentlessly seek to improve our performance. We bring urgency to every business challenge and opportunity. We anticipate change and shape it to our purpose. We encourage new ideas that challenge the status quo, and we seek to involve every mind in the growth of our business.

Personal integrity. We at BorgWarner demand uncompromising ethical standards in all we do and say. We are committed to doing what is right—in good times and in bad. We are accountable for the commitments we make. We are, above all, an honorable company of honorable people.

Responsibility to our communities. BorgWarner is committed to good corporate citizenship. We strive to supply goods and services of superior value to our customers; to create jobs that provide meaning for those who do them; and to contribute generously of our talents and our wealth in the communities in which we do business.

CORPORATE DESCRIPTION
Auburn Hills, Michigan-based BorgWarner Inc. (NYSE: BWA) is a product leader in highly engineered components and systems for vehicle power-train applications worldwide. The company operates manufacturing and technical facilities in sixty-two locations in seventeen countries.

ADDRESS
3850 Hamlin Road
Auburn Hills, MI 48326
www.borgwarner.com

CAMPBELL SOUP COMPANY

OUR MISSION

Together we will build the world's most extraordinary food company.

OUR VISION

Nourishing people's lives, everywhere, every day.

OUR WAY

We will combine the power of our icon brands, our competitive advantages in simple meals and baked snacks, and our talented people to drive quality growth.

CORPORATE DESCRIPTION

Campbell Soup Company is a global manufacturer of high quality soup, beverage, confectionery, and prepared food products. The company is 136 years old with over $7 billion in annual sales and a portfolio of more than twenty market-leading brands.

ADDRESS

One Campbell Place
Camden, NJ 08103
www.campbellsoup.com

CHIQUITA BRANDS INTERNATIONAL, INC.

VISION

Chiquita will be one of the most respected companies in the world, consistently delivering sustainable, profitable growth by committed, passionate, and disciplined professionals, while maintaining high standards and conservative financial policies.

MISSION

To be a consumer-driven global leader of branded and value-added produce. We will win the hearts and smiles of the world's consumers by helping them enjoy nutritional and healthy products.

CORPORATE DESCRIPTION

Chiquita Brands International, Inc. is a leading international marketer and distributor of high-quality fresh and value-added produce such as fresh-cut fruit, which is sold under the Chiquita premium brand and other trademarks. The company is one of the largest banana producers in the world and a major supplier of bananas in Europe and North America.

ADDRESS

250 East Fifth Street
Cincinnati, OH 45202
www.chiquita.com

CHIRON CORPORATION

VISION
To create value by transforming the practice of medicine through bio-technology.

MISSION
Protecting people through innovative science by:
- Working to cure cancer
- Providing safe blood
- Preventing infectious diseases

VALUES
- Transparency
- Alignment
- Execution
- Accountability

CORPORATE DESCRIPTION
Chiron is a business unit of Novartis Vaccines and Diagnostics, a new division of Novartis focused on the development of preventative treatments and tools. (See www.novartis.com). Dedicated to preventing transfusion-transmitted diseases, Chiron delivers innovative blood-screening tools, products, and services to protect the world's blood supply. Beginning with the sequencing of the HIV genome in 1984 and the discovery of the hepatitis C genome in 1987, Chiron has been a consistent leader in making groundbreaking discoveries and developing innovative solutions for preventing and treating infectious diseases.

ADDRESS
4560 Horton Street
Emeryville, CA 94608
www.chiron.com

CLEAR CHANNEL COMMUNICATIONS

MISSION

To provide outstanding entertainment and information products and ser-vices to our communities and effective solutions to advertisers.

Note: Please see the company website for its comprehensive Creed Statement.

CORPORATE DESCRIPTION

Clear Channel Communications is a diversified media company.

ADDRESS

200 East Basse Road
San Antonio, TX 78209
www.clearchannel.com

COCA-COLA COMPANY

THE COCA-COLA PROMISE
The Coca-Cola Company exists to benefit and refresh everyone it touches.
The basic proposition of our business is simple, solid, and timeless.
When we bring refreshment, value, joy and fun to our stakeholders, then
we successfully nurture and protect our brands, particularly Coca-Cola.
That is the key to fulfilling our ultimate obligation to provide consistently
attractive returns to the owners of our business.

CORPORATE DESCRIPTION
The Coca-Cola Company is the largest manufacturer, distributor, and marketer of nonalcoholic beverage concentrates and syrups in the world.

ADDRESS
One Coca-Cola Plaza
Atlanta, GA 30313
www.cocacola.com

COMCAST CORPORATION

THE COMCAST CREDO

We will be the company to look to first for the communications products and services that connect people to what's important in their lives.

CORPORATE DESCRIPTION

Comcast Corporation is the nation's leading provider of cable, entertainment and communications products and services. Comcast is principally involved in the development, management and operation of broadband cable networks and in the delivery of programming content.

ADDRESS

1500 Market Street
Philadelphia, PA 19102
www.comcast.com

CONAGRA FOODS, INC.

VISION

One company growing by nourishing lives
and finding a better way today
. . . one bite at a time!

CORPORATE DESCRIPTION

ConAgra Foods, Inc. (NYSE: CAG) is one of North America's leading packaged foods companies with a strong presence in consumer grocery as well as restaurant and foodservice establishments.

ADDRESS

One ConAgra Drive
Omaha, NE 68102
www.conagrafoods.com

DEERE & COMPANY

JOHN DEERE STRATEGY

We aspire to distinctively serve customers—those linked to the land—through a great business, a business as great as our products. To achieve this aspiration, our strategy is:

- Exceptional operating performance
- Disciplined SVA growth
- Aligned, high-performance teamwork

Execution of this strategy creates the distinctive John Deere Experience that ultimately propels a great business and, for all with a stake in our success, delivers Performance That Endures.

CORPORATE DESCRIPTION

John Deere (Deere & Company—NYSE: DE) is the world's leading manufacturer of agricultural and forestry equipment; a leading supplier of equipment used in lawn, grounds and turf care; and a major manufacturer of construction equipment. Additionally, John Deere manufactures engines used in heavy equipment and provides financial services and other related activities that support the core businesses. Since it was first founded in 1837, the company has established a heritage of quality products and services providing performance that endures to customers worldwide.

ADDRESS

One John Deere Place
Moline, IL 61265
www.deere.com

DEL MONTE FOODS

VISION

Del Monte. Nourishing families. Enriching lives.

MISSION

Del Monte is committed to enriching the lives of today's family—everyone in the family, including pets—by providing nourishing, great tasting, and easy-to-use products that meet the needs of everyone in the home. We are driven by the consumer and deliver results through a partnership with our customers built upon superior brands and products, continuous innovation, excellent service, and a commitment to quality in all we do. Our people are passionate about winning and take pride in Del Monte as they lead the company to achieve world-class performance and superior shareholder value.

CORPORATE DESCRIPTION

Del Monte Foods Company (NYSE: DLM) is one of the country's largest and most well-known producers, distributors and marketers of premium quality, branded and private label food and pet products for the U.S. retail market, generating over $3 billion in net sales in fiscal year 2005. With a powerful portfolio of brands including Del Monte®, Contadina®, StarKist®, S&W®, *Nature's Goodness™,* College Inn®, 9Lives®, Kibbles 'n Bits®, Pup-Peroni®, Snausages®, Pounce®, and Meaty Bone®, Del Monte products are found in nine out of ten American households.

ADDRESS

One Market @ The Landmark
P.O. Box 193575
San Francisco, CA 94119
www.delmonte.com

DENNY'S CORPORATION

VISION STATEMENT
Great Food and Great Service by Great People...Every Time!

MISSION STATEMENT
Our mission is to profitably grow the company by providing our guests with great food, service and hospitality in a clean, comfortable restaurant, twenty-four hours a day.

CORE VALUES
Our Core Values bind us together as a company through a code of shared beliefs. These beliefs guide our actions and decisions, forming the culture of our company.

Giving Our Best. Our passion for doing our best is reflected in everything we do. We step up, reach out, pitch in, and find ways to go above and beyond to extend the hospitality and service that are fundamental to our business.

Appreciating Others. Our diversity is part of who we are. We recognize the value of different approaches, thinking, perspectives, and people. We share similarities in our combined efforts to achieve our goals, but we are uniquely different—and therein lies our strength.

A Can-Do Attitude. Because we are always "on," we have developed the toughness and endurance with our business that never stops. We are resilient when faced with obstacles; constantly looking for ways to say "yes," and proud of being part of the marathon team in family dining.

DENNY'S CORPORATION (CONTINUED)

CORPORATE DESCRIPTION

Denny's is America's largest full-service family restaurant chain, consisting of 547 company-owned units and 1,036 franchised and licensed units, with operations in the United States, Canada, Costa Rica, Guam, Mexico, New Zealand and Puerto Rico.

ADDRESS

203 East Main Street
Spartanburg, SC 29319
www.dennys.com

DOLLAR GENERAL CORPORATION

OUR MISSION
Serving Others
For Customers...A Better Life
For Shareholders...A Superior Return
For Employees...Respect and Opportunity

Note: Please refer to the company's website to see its statement of Strategy and Values.

CORPORATE DESCRIPTION
Founded in 1939 as J.L. Turner & Son, a wholesale business in Scottsville, Kentucky, Dollar General (NYSE: DG) is a *Fortune* 500 company and the leader in the dollar store segment, with more than 8,000 stores and $7.6 billion in annual sales. The company pioneered the dollar store concept in 1955, opening retail stores that sold all items for $1. The format was extremely successful, boosting the company's sales to $25.8 million by 1965. A few years later in 1968, the company launched its initial public stock offering and changed its name to Dollar General.

ADDRESS
100 Mission Ridge
Goodlettsville, TN 37072
www.dollargeneral.com

DREYER'S GRAND ICE CREAM HOLDINGS, INC.

MISSION STATEMENT
To become the pre-eminent ice cream company in the United States.

CORPORATE DESCRIPTION
Dreyer's Grand Ice Cream Holdings, Inc. and its subsidiaries manufacture and distribute a full spectrum of ice cream and frozen dessert products. Brands of frozen dessert products currently manufactured or distributed by Dreyer's in the United States include Grand, Grand Light®, Slow Churned™ Light, Häagen-Dazs®, Häagen-Dazs® Light, Dibs™, Nestlé® Drumstick®, Nestlé Crunch®, Butterfinger®, Toll House®, Carnation®, Push-Up®, Dole®, Homemade, Fruit Bars, Starbucks®, Skinny Cow®, Skinny Carb Bar™ and Healthy Choice®. The company's premium products are marketed under the Dreyer's brand name throughout the western states and Texas, and under the Edy's name throughout the remainder of the United States.

Edy's, the Dreyer's and Edy's logo design, Slow Churned and Homemade, are all trademarks or trade names of Dreyer's Grand Ice Cream, Inc. The Nestlé and Häagen-Dazs trademarks in the U.S. are licensed to Dreyer's by Nestlé. All other trademarks and trade names are owned by their respective companies and licensed to Dreyer's. NESTLÉ® DRUMSTICK®, NESTLÉ CRUNCH®, BUTTERFINGER®, TOLL HOUSE®, CARNATION and PUSH-UP® are registered trademarks of Société de Produits Nestlé S.A., Vevey, Switzerland.

ADDRESS
5929 College Avenue
Oakland, CA 94618
www.dreyers.com

EATON CORPORATION

MISSION STATEMENT

To be our customers' best supplier, providing distinctive and highly valued products, services and solutions.

EATON VALUES: THE FOUNDATION FOR CONTINUED SUCCESS

As a corporation owned by shareholders, Eaton's fundamental purpose—the reason the Company exists—is to operate profitably, to provide an attractive return for those who have invested in us, and increase shareholder value. Throughout our long history, we have come to understand that our ability to achieve these business goals depends on our adherence to Eaton's core values:

- Make our customers the focus of everything we do
- Recognize our people as our greatest asset
- Treat each other with respect
- Be fair, honest, and open
- Be considerate of the environment and our communities
- Keep our commitments
- Strive for excellence

CORPORATE DESCRIPTION

Eaton Corporation is a diversified industrial manufacturer. Eaton is a global leader in electrical systems and components for power quality, distribution, and control; fluid power systems and services for industrial, mobile, and aircraft equipment; intelligent truck drivetrain systems for safety and fuel economy; and automotive engine air management systems, powertrain solutions, and specialty controls for performance, fuel economy and safety. Eaton has 59,000 employees and sells products to customers in more than 125 countries.

EATON CORPORATION

ADDRESS

1111 Superior Avenue
Cleveland, OH 44114
www.eaton.com

ECOLAB

OUR MISSION

Our mission is to be the leading global innovator, developer, and provider of cleaning, sanitation, and maintenance products, systems, and services. As a team, we will achieve aggressive growth and a fair return for our shareholders. We will accomplish this by exceeding the expectations of our customers while conserving resources and preserving the quality of the environment.

Note: Please refer to the company website to see its extensive Quest for Excellence and The Ecolab Culture statements.

CORPORATE DESCRIPTION

Ecolab is the global leader in premium cleaning, sanitizing, pest elimination, maintenance, and repair products and services for the world's hospitality, foodservice, institutional, and industrial markets. Customers include hotels and restaurants; healthcare and educational facilities; grocery stores; commercial laundries; light industry; dairy plants and farms; and food and beverage processors.

ADDRESS

Ecolab Center
370 North Wabasha Street
St. Paul, MN 55102
www.ecolab.com

FEDERATED DEPARTMENT STORES, INC.

CORPORATE PHILOSOPHY

Federated clearly recognizes that the customer is paramount, and that all actions and strategies must be directed toward providing an enhanced merchandise offering and better service to targeted consumers through dynamic department stores and direct-to-customer retail formats.

Aggressive implementation of the company's strategies, as well as careful and thorough planning, will provide Federated's department stores with an important competitive edge.

Federated is committed to open and honest communications with employees, shareholders, vendors, customers, analysts, and the news media. The company seeks to be proactive in sharing information and in keeping these key stakeholder groups up-to-date on important and material developments.

At Federated, our greatest strength lies in the skill, judgment and talent of our people. Every day a production of enormous magnitude takes place on our selling floors and behind the scenes, where our people bring the company's strategic goals to life. Our priority on attracting, retaining, and growing the most talented people in the retail industry has been and will continue to be our greatest advantage.

CORPORATE OBJECTIVES

The corporate objectives of Federated Department Stores, Inc. are:

- To accelerate comparable store sales growth;
- To effectively utilize excess cash flow through a combination of strategic growth opportunities, stock buybacks, debt reduction, and dividend payments
- To grow earnings per share while increasing return on gross investment; and
- To continue to increase the company's profitability levels (earnings before interest, taxes, depreciation, and amortization) as a percent of sales.

CORPORATE DESCRIPTION

Federated Department Stores, Inc. is one of the nation's leading retailers. Federated operated 866 stores in forty-five states, the District of Columbia, Guam and Puerto Rico as of January 28, 2006 under the names of Macy's, Bloomingdale's, Famous-Barr, Filene's, Foley's, Hecht's, Kaufmann's, L.S. Ayres, Marshall Field's, Meier & Frank, Robinsons-May, Strawbridge's, and The Jones Store. Federated also operates macys.com, bloomingdales.com and Bloomingdale's By Mail. Federated also operated fifty-six Lord & Taylor and 735 bridal and formalwear stores in forty-seven states and Puerto Rico as of January 28, 2006 under the names of David's Bridal, After Hours Formalwear and Priscilla of Boston.

ADDRESS

7 West Seventh Street
Cincinnati, OH 45202
www.federated-fds.com

FIRST HORIZON
NATIONAL CORPORATION

OUR VISION

A premier national financial services company, dedicated to creating the highest levels of value, producing long-term levels of industry leading profitability and growth.

OUR SIX CORE VALUES

Employees first. We hire, retain and develop the best people, ensuring that every employee has the opportunity to demonstrate high performance and succeed. Also, we'll nurture our Firstpower culture as our competitive advantage.

Exceptional teamwork. As one enterprise, we exhibit an uncommon ability to work together, based on interdependence and trust.

Individual accountability. As owners, we take individual responsibility for our overall success.

Absolute determination. When we identify a goal, we are committed to getting it done. We execute with speed and diligence and take pride in going above and beyond.

Knowing our customers. We create value and build loyalty by understanding and exceeding the expectations of customers in our target markets.

Doing the right thing. We have the courage to make decisions and take actions based on personal and professional integrity.

CORPORATE DESCRIPTION

The 13,000 employees of First Horizon National Corporation provide financial services to individuals and business customers through hundreds of offices located in more than forty states. The corporation's three major brands—FTN Financial, First Horizon and First Tennessee—provide customers with a broad range of products and services including capital markets, mortgage banking, and retail and commercial banking.

ADDRESS

165 Madison Avenue
Memphis, TN 38103
www.fhnc.com

FOREMOST FARMS USA

Foremost Farms USA Cooperative will successfully operate in the dynamic food and beverage marketplace to grow a financially sound business which will be the market of choice for dairy producers.

STATEMENT OF PURPOSE
Foremost Farms USA Cooperative will provide dairy producers a financially strong business that efficiently assembles, processes, and markets milk and related dairy products providing superior value to our customers in a manner that generates fair and equitable returns for present, past, and future member/owners.

BELIEFS AND VALUES
• We believe that our member/owners' expectations and return on investment are maximized by being market driven and by engaging all employees in business improvement activities.

• We believe that honesty, integrity, and respect in our relationships with our customers, member/owners, employees, and vendors, is of the highest importance and will not be compromised.

• We believe that most people want to do the right thing, want to contribute, want to do quality work, want to have a positive impact and will if the system enables them to do so.

• We believe that every employee has unique skills, knowledge, and experience that make them important to Foremost Farms USA Cooperative.

• We believe that respectfully, constructively, and creatively challenging the status quo is fundamental to our future success.

• Customer satisfaction, efficient and safe operations, and profitability are the priority and focus of all employees, rather than what might be optimal for an individual function or operation.

• We believe in acting in a responsible and ethical manner in our relations with our communities and the general public.

• We will ensure a safe and healthy workplace, with all employees being properly trained and equipped, and accountable for working in a safe and healthy manner.

CORPORATE DESCRIPTION

Foremost Farms USA is among the top ten dairy cooperatives in the United States, owned by about 3,760 dairy farmer/members in Illinois, Indiana, Iowa, Michigan, Minnesota, Ohio, and Wisconsin.

ADDRESS

E10889A Penny Lane
P.O. Box 111
Baraboo, WI 53913
www.foremostfarms.com

FPL GROUP, INC.

CORPORATE VISION

We will be the preferred provider of safe, reliable, and cost-effective products and services that satisfy the electricity-related needs of all customer segments.

CORPORATE DESCRIPTION

FPL Group, with annual revenues of more than $10.5 billion, is nationally known as a high-quality, efficient, and customer-driven organization focused on energy-related products and services. With a growing presence in twenty-six states, it is widely recognized as one of the country's premier power companies. Its principal subsidiary, Florida Power & Light Company, serves more than 4.2 million customer accounts in Florida. FPL Energy, LLC, FPL Group's wholesale generating subsidiary, is a leader in producing electricity from clean and renewable fuels.

ADDRESS

700 Universe Boulevard
P.O. Box 14000
Juno Beach, FL 33408
www.fpl.com

GENERAL MOTORS CORPORATION

GM'S VISION

GM's vision is to be the world leader in transportation products and related services. We will earn our customers' enthusiasm through continuous improvement driven by the integrity, teamwork, and innovation of GM people.

CORE VALUES

Core values are what our company stands for and are shared by everyone throughout the organization.

Customer Enthusiasm. We will dedicate ourselves to products and services that create enthusiastic customers. No one will be second-guessed for doing the right thing for the customer.

Integrity. We will stand for honesty and trust in everything we do. We will say what we believe and do what we say.

Teamwork. We will win by thinking and acting together as one General Motors team, focused on global leadership. Our strengths are our highly skilled people and our diversity.

Innovation. We will challenge conventional thinking, explore new technology and implement new ideas regardless of their source faster than our competition.

Continuous Improvement. We will set ambitious goals, stretch to meet them, and then "raise the bar" again and again. We believe that everything can be done better, faster, and more effectively in a learning environment.

Individual Respect and Responsibility. We will respect others and act responsibly, so that we can work together to meet our common goals.

GENERAL MOTORS
CORPORATION (CONTINUED)

CORPORATE DESCRIPTION

General Motors Corporation (NYSE: GM), the world's largest automaker, has been the global industry sales leader since 1931. Founded in 1908, GM today employs approximately 325,000 people around the world. It has manufacturing operations in 32 countries and its vehicles are sold in 200 countries.

ADDRESS

300 Renaissance Center
Detroit, MI 48265
www.gm.com

GILLETTE

OUR VISION

The Gillette Company's Vision is to build Total Brand Value by innovating to deliver consumer value and customer leadership faster, better, and more completely than our competition. This Vision is supported by two fundamental principles that provide the foundation for all of our activities: Organizational Excellence and Core Values.

ORGANIZATIONAL EXCELLENCE

Attaining our Vision requires superior and continually improving performance in every area and at every level of the organization. Our performance will be guided by a clear and concise strategic statement for each business unit and by an ongoing Quest for Excellence within all operational and staff functions. This Quest for Excellence requires hiring, developing and retaining a diverse workforce of the highest caliber. To support this Quest, each function employs metrics to define, and implements processes to achieve, world-class status.

CORE VALUES

As we work toward our Vision, three core Values define the way we operate:

Achievement. We are dedicated to the highest standards of achievement in all areas of our business. We strive to consistently exceed the expectations of both external and internal customers.

Integrity. Mutual respect and ethical behavior are the basis for our relationships with colleagues, customers and the community. Fair practice is the hallmark of the Company.

Collaboration. We work closely together as one global team to improve the way we do business every day. We communicate openly and establish clear accountability for making decisions, identifying issues and solutions, and maximizing business opportunities.

GILLETTE (CONTINUED)

CORPORATE DESCRIPTION

The Gillette Company is the world leader in male grooming products, a category that includes blades, razors, and shaving preparations. Gillette also holds the number-one position worldwide in selected female grooming products, such as wet shaving products and hair epilation devices. In addition, the company is the world leader in alkaline batteries, and manual and power toothbrushes. Gillette is proud to be a part of the Procter & Gamble family of brands that make everyday life just a little bit better.

ADDRESS

P.O. Box 599
Cincinnati, OH 45201
www.gillette.com

GRACE (W.R. GRACE & CO.)

OUR VISION

Grace will be a premier specialty chemicals and materials company applying innovative technologies to provide value-added products and services to global markets.

OUR VALUES

The Grace values serve as the blueprint for how we do business.

People and Teamwork: Treat each other with respect; together, we are stronger. Work effectively with each other to win the marketplace. Hold people accountable for their actions. Encourage initiative. Recognize accomplishments. Work together across businesses and around the world sharing knowledge and best practices. Communicate openly and candidly.

Customers and Performance: Provide products and services that will make our customers successful with their customers. Set high expectations for everything we do and meet our commitments.

Integrity and Ethics: Maintain and expect the highest level of ethical behavior. Obey laws, report financial results accurately and protect the environment. Operate safely and responsibly around the world.

Agility and Speed: Challenge complexity and reduce bureaucracy. Move quickly to seize advantages in the marketplace. Anticipate shifts in markets and respond to our competitors.

Innovation and Creativity: Encourage people to constantly look for new ways to create value for our customers. Accept change as an opportunity and use it to our advantage.

CORPORATE DESCRIPTION

Grace is a global supplier of catalysts and other products and services to petroleum refiners; catalysts for the manufacturer of plastics; silica-based engineered and specialty materials for a wide range of industrial applications; specialty chemicals, additives, and materials for commercial and residential construction; and can sealants and coatings for food packaging.

ADDRESS
7500 Grace Drive
Columbia, MD 21044
www.grace.com

HAWORTH INC.

VISION
At Haworth, we create beautiful, effective, and adaptable workplaces.

VALUES
We value our customers. We believe each customer is special. We listen closely to their needs and, with our dealers, collaborate to create great spaces. With passion, we combine our energy, knowledge, and talents daily to manufacture goods and services that exceed our customers' expectations.

We value members. We believe in the boundless potential of people empowered, engaged, and focused on a common vision.

Haworth is composed of people from all parts of the world, giving us a rich breadth of experience, cultural backgrounds, depth of talent, and human potential. We build on the diversity of our members and dedicate ourselves to developing a culture that encourages and appreciates the contributions of each individual.

We value and celebrate our differences, yet we are united by our desire to be the best.

We value integrity. We believe that honesty and candor are the foundation for integrity and trust. We build mutually beneficial relationships with our customers, architects, designers, dealers, members, and suppliers.

We value continuous learning. We believe that knowledge empowers and learning leads to change and growth of individuals and organizations. In our drive for continuous improvement, we encourage our members to take risks, look for smarter ways to work, seek new ideas, reduce waste, and use resources wisely.

HAWORTH INC.

We value results. We design, market, manufacture, and deliver products and services to meet the most stringent design and quality standards—those of our customers.

We admire competence, seek best practices, and strive for swift execution. In a complex business, we strive for simplicity and clarity of purpose, valuing a job done right.

We enjoy working together and take pride in our work and our company.

We value our world. We think beyond our business to our communities. We cultivate hope for our future by investing in people, education, and a sustainable world. In our small way, we will help make the world a better place for people to work and live.

CORPORATE DESCRIPTION

Haworth Inc. is a global leader in the design and manufacture of adaptable workplaces, including raised floors, movable walls, systems furniture, seating, storage, and wood casegoods. Family-owned and privately held, Haworth is headquartered in Holland, Michigan, and serves markets in more than 120 countries through a global network of 600 dealers. The company had net sales of US $1.4 billion in 2005.

ADDRESS

One Haworth Center
Holland, MI 49423
www.haworth.com

HCA INC. (HOSPITAL CORPORATION OF AMERICA)

MISSION & VISION / *HEART—CARING FOR YOU*

Above all else, we are committed to the care and improvement of human life. In recognition of this commitment, we strive to deliver high-quality, cost-effective health care in the communities we serve.

In pursuit of our mission, we believe the following value statements are essential and timeless.

We recognize and affirm the unique and intrinsic worth of each individual.

We treat all those we serve with compassion and kindness.

We act with absolute honesty, integrity, and fairness in the way we conduct our business and the way we live our lives.

We trust our colleagues as valuable members of our healthcare team and pledge to treat one another with loyalty, respect and dignity.

CORPORATE DESCRIPTION

HCA Inc. owns and operates approximately 182 hospitals and approximately 94 freestanding surgery centers in twenty-two states, with additional centers in England and Switzerland.

ADDRESS

One Park Plaza
Nashville, TN 37203
www.hcahealthcare.com

HERSHEY'S (THE HERSHEY COMPANY)

MISSION

Undisputed Marketplace Leadership

- Top-tier value creation, driven by superior performance across the business system
- Organizational capabilities and passion that compete in the present and build for the future
- Commitment to enabling and encouraging balanced, healthy lives
- Portfolio of brands that:
    Delights consumers across multiple segments
    Delivers superior growth and profitability to retailers
    Is available everywhere
- Ability to transform consumer and customer desires to marketplace wins

CORPORATE DESCRIPTION

The Hershey Company (NYSE: HSY) is a leading snack food company and the largest North American manufacturer of quality chocolate and nonchocolate confectionery products, with revenues of over $4 billion and more than 13,000 employees worldwide.

ADDRESS

100 Crystal A Drive
P.O. Box 810
Hershey, PA 17033
www.hersheys.com

HEWITT ASSOCIATES

MISSION
Making the world a better place to work

VALUES

People: We treat one another, our clients, participants, business partners, and suppliers with respect and dignity. We build positive relationships through open communication, sharing, and valuing diverse perspectives.

Excellence: We all share the responsibility to deliver to clients solutions that demonstrate quality, reliability, and innovation in our work. We achieve excellence in what we do through personal initiative and continuous development of skills and knowledge, with strong support from the company.

Collaboration/Teamwork: Teamwork unites our individual talents to serve our clients and their people exceptionally well. Working together, we can leverage individual ideas and contributions into a greater result benefiting clients, other associates, our company, our business partners, and our service providers.

Integrity: Ethical behavior, honesty, and integrity are fundamental characteristics of our conduct in all aspects of our work.

CORPORATE DESCRIPTION
With more than sixty years of experience, Hewitt Associates (NYSE: HEW) is the world's foremost provider of human resources outsourcing and consulting services. The company consults with more than 2,400 organizations and administers human resources, health care, payroll, and retirement programs on behalf of more than 350 companies to millions of employees and retirees worldwide. Located in thirty-five countries, Hewitt employs approximately 22,000 associates.

HEWITT ASSOCIATES (CONTINUED)

ADDRESS
100 Half Day Road
Lincolnshire, IL 60069
www.hewitt.com

HOLLY CORPORATION

MISSION STATEMENT

Our mission is to be a premier U.S. petroleum refining, pipeline, and terminal company as measured by superior financial performance and sustainable, profitable growth.

We seek to accomplish this by operating safely, reliably, and in an environmentally responsible manner; effectively and efficiently operating our existing assets; offering superior products and services; and growing organically and through strategic acquisitions.

We strive to outperform our competition due to the quality and development of our people and our assets. We endeavor to maintain an inclusive and stimulating work environment that enables each employee to fully contribute to and participate in the Company's success.

CORPORATE DESCRIPTION

Holly Corporation is principally an independent petroleum refiner that produces high-value light products such as gasoline, diesel fuel, and jet fuel.

ADDRESS

100 Crescent Court
Suite 1600
Dallas, TX 75201
www.hollycorp.com

HONEYWELL
INTERNATIONAL, INC.

OUR BRAND PROMISE

We are building a world that's safer and more secure...more comfortable and energy efficient...more innovative and productive. We are Honeywell.

OUR MISSION

For our customers: To develop technologies and innovations that improve the competitive landscape for them and their customers.

For our shareowners: To deliver consistent earnings growth, competitive returns on investment, and superior financial performance driven by customer satisfaction and leadership in high-growth industries.

OUR VALUES

The company's 120,000 employees throughout more than 100 countries focus daily on the Five Initiatives—Growth, Productivity, Cash, People and our Enablers, Honeywell Operating System, Functional Transformation and Velocity Product Development™—to best serve customers and ensure Honeywell's long-term success. They are guided in their actions by a common set of expectations called the Twelve Behaviors: Growth and Customer Focus, Leadership Impact, Gets Results, Makes People Better, Champions of Change and Six Sigma, Fosters Teamwork and Diversity, Global Mindset, Intelligent Risk Taking, Self-Aware/Learner, Effective Communicator, Integrative Thinker and Technical or Functional Excellence.

CORPORATE DESCRIPTION

Honeywell International, Inc. is a $28 billion diversified technology and manufacturing leader, serving customers worldwide with aerospace products and services; control technologies for buildings, homes, and industry; automotive products; turbochargers; and specialty materials.

ADDRESS

101 Columbia Road
Morristown, NJ 07962
www.honeywell.com

IBM (INTERNATIONAL BUSINESS MACHINES CORPORATION)

MISSION STATEMENT
The company's business model is built to support two principal goals: helping clients succeed in delivering business value by becoming more efficient and competitive through the use of business insight and information technology (IT) solutions; and providing long-term value to shareholders. In support of these objectives, the business model has been developed over time through strategic investments in services and technologies that have the best long-term growth and profitability prospects based on the value they deliver to clients. In addition, the company is committed to its employees and the communities in which it operates.

CORPORATE DESCRIPTION
"At IBM, we strive to lead in the invention, development and manufacture of the industry's most advanced information technologies, including computer systems, software, storage systems and microelectronics. We translate these advanced technologies into value for our customers through our professional solutions, services and consulting businesses worldwide."

— From "About IBM" at www.ibm.com

ADDRESS
New Orchard Road
Armonk, NY 10504
www.ibm.com

INGERSOLL-RAND

OUR VISION

We are dedicated to driving shareholder value by achieving:

Dramatic Growth—By focusing on innovative solutions for our customers

Operational Excellence—By pursuing continuous improvement in all our operations

Dual Citizenship—By bringing together the talents, energy, and enthusiasm of all Ingersoll-Rand people

OUR VALUES

Collaboration—The collaboration between the employees of Ingersoll-Sergeant and Rand Drill, who joined forces to build Ingersoll-Rand.

Courage—The courage shown by Addison and Jasper Rand to leave their family's successful buggy whip business.

Innovation—The innovation demonstrated by Simon Ingersoll, Henry Clark Sergeant, Frederick McKinley Jones, Walter Schlage, and so many others.

Integrity—The integrity shown by Michael P. Grace when he had the original merger agreement changed to better serve shareholders.

Respect—The respect for our employees, customers, and communities that has enabled Ingersoll-Rand to thrive and grow over the past 100 years.

CORPORATE DESCRIPTION

Ingersoll-Rand is a global provider of products, services, and integrated solutions to industries as diverse as transportation, manufacturing, construction, security, and agriculture. The company features a portfolio of worldwide businesses comprising an enviable roster of leading industrial

INGERSOLL-RAND (CONTINUED)

and commercial brands, such as Bobcat compact equipment, Club Car golf cars, Hussman stationary refrigeration equipment, Ingersoll-Rand industrial and construction equipment, Schlage locks, and Thermo King transport temperature-control equipment.

ADDRESS
155 Chestnut Ridge Road
P.O. Box 0445
Montvale, NJ 07645
www.ingersollrand.com

INTERNATIONAL GAME TECHNOLOGY (IGT)

MISSION STATEMENT

IGT is in business to provide for the needs of our customers, our employees, and our shareholders, while recognizing our responsibility to the communities in which we operate.

• IGT is committed to providing our customers with quality products at a competitive price which, together with excellent service and support, will assist them in maximizing their profitability.

• IGT is committed to providing our employees with a stable and rewarding work environment, the opportunity to grow to the extent of their talents, and the opportunity to share in the success of the company which they make possible.

• IGT is committed to providing our shareholders with an above-average return on their investment, since our ability to serve the needs of our customers and employees is made possible only through their support.

• IGT is committed to being a responsible corporate citizen in the communities in which we operate, and encourages our employees to individually be an asset to the community in which they live.

CORPORATE DESCRIPTION

International Game Technology (www.IGT.com) is a global company specializing in the design, development, manufacturing, distribution and sales of computerized gaming machines and systems products.

ADDRESS

9295 Prototype Drive
Reno, NV 89521
www.igt.com

INTERNATIONAL PAPER COMPANY

OUR VISION—WHAT WE WANT TO BECOME

International Paper will be one of the best and most respected companies in the world—as measured by our employees, our customers, our communities, and our shareholders.

OUR MISSION—WHY WE EXIST, WHAT WE DO, AND HOW WE DO IT

International Paper is dedicated to making people's lives better.

- Our employees use renewable resources to make products people depend on every day.

- Our customers succeed because our innovative products and services make their businesses better.

- Our communities welcome us as neighbors, employers, and environmental stewards.

- Our shareholders benefit from our superior financial performances.

- By keeping our promises, we deliver results.

CORPORATE DESCRIPTION

Headquartered in the United States, International Paper Company is the world's largest paper and forest products company, with offices located primarily in North America, Europe, Asia and Latin America. Key businesses include uncoated papers, packaging, and distribution.

ADDRESS

400 Atlantic Street
Stamford, CT 06921
www.internationalpaper.com

JOHNSON & JOHNSON

OUR COMPANY

At Johnson & Johnson there is no mission statement that hangs on the wall. Instead, for more than sixty years, a simple, one-page document—Our Credo—has guided our actions in fulfilling our responsibilities to our customers, our employees, the community and our stockholders.

OUR CREDO

We believe our first responsibility is to the doctors,
nurses, and patients,
to mothers and fathers, and all others who use our
products and services.
In meeting their needs everything we do must be of
high quality.
We must constantly strive to reduce our costs
in order to maintain reasonable prices.
Customers' orders must be serviced promptly and
accurately.
Our suppliers and distributors must have an opportunity
to make a fair profit.

We are responsible to our employees,
the men and women who work with us throughout the
world.
Everyone must be considered as an individual.
We must respect their dignity and recognize their merit.
They must have a sense of security in their jobs.
Compensation must be fair and adequate,
and working conditions clean, orderly and safe.
We must be mindful of ways to help our employees
fulfill
their family responsibilities.

Employees must feel free to make suggestions and
complaints.
There must be equal opportunity for employment,
development
and advancement for those qualified.
We must provide competent management,
and their actions must be just and ethical.

We are responsible to the communities in which we live
and work
and to the world community as well.
We must be good citizens—support good works and
charities
and bear our fair share of taxes.
We must encourage civic improvements and better
health and education.
We must maintain in good order
the property we are privileged to use,
protecting the environment and natural resources.

Our final responsibility is to our stockholders.
Business must make a sound profit.
We must experiment with new ideas.
Research must be carried on, innovative programs
developed
and mistakes paid for.
New equipment must be purchased, new facilities
provided
and new products launched.
Reserves must be created to provide for adverse times.
When we operate according to these principles,
the stockholders should realize a fair return.

CORPORATE DESCRIPTION

Johnson & Johnson, through its operating companies, is the world's most comprehensive and broadly based manufacturer of health care products, as well as a provider of related services, for the consumer, pharmaceutical, and medical devices and diagnostics markets.

ADDRESS

One Johnson & Johnson Plaza
New Brunswick, NJ 08933
www.jnj.com

JOHNSON CONTROLS, INC.

OUR CREED

We believe in the free enterprise system. We shall consistently treat our customers, employees, shareholders, suppliers and the community with honesty, dignity, fairness and respect. We will conduct our business with the highest ethical standards.

OUR MISSION

Continually exceed our customers' increasing expectations.

Note: Please refer to the company's website for the entire series of company statements under the umbrella Vision Statement. These statements include Our Creed and Our Mission cited above, plus statements of What We Value and Objectives.

CORPORATE DESCRIPTION

Johnson Controls, Inc. (NYSE: JCI) is a global market leader in automotive systems and facility management and control. In the automotive market, it is a major supplier of integrated seating and interior systems, and batteries. For nonresidential facilities, Johnson Controls provides control systems and services including comfort, energy and security management.

ADDRESS

5757 North Green Bay Avenue
Milwaukee, WI 53209
www.jci.com

KANSAS CITY LIFE
INSURANCE COMPANY

PURPOSE OF KANSAS CITY LIFE INSURANCE COMPANY

Kansas City Life Insurance Company exists to provide present and future financial security to people, thereby assuring them a dignity and a quality of life that they and their beneficiaries might otherwise not enjoy, and to sustain Kansas City Life's own growth and prosperity through good management and reasonable profit, thus enabling the Company to continue to serve people for as long as their needs exist.

Note: Please refer to the company's website to see the company's Business Philosophies statement that accompanies the statement of Purpose.

CORPORATE DESCRIPTION

Kansas City Life Insurance Company markets individual life, annuity and group products through general agencies located throughout the United States. Variable life, variable annuities, mutual funds and other investment options are offered through Sunset Financial Services, Kansas City Life's wholly-owned broker/dealer subsidiary.

ADDRESS

3520 Broadway
Kansas City, MO 64111
www.kclife.com

KELLOGG COMPANY

OUR IDENTITY
We build *Gr-r-reat* brands and make the world a little happier by bringing our best to you.

OUR MISSION
Kellogg is a global company committed to building long-term growth and to enhancing our worldwide leadership position by providing nutritious food products of superior value. As our founder, W.K. Kellogg, once described us, "We are a company of dedicated people making quality products for a healthier world."

Note: Please refer to the company's website for its extensive series of company statements including Our Working Environment plus Our Shared Values and Our Beliefs.

CORPORATE DESCRIPTION
Kellogg Company is the world's leading producer of cereal and a leading producer of convenience foods, including cookies, crackers, toaster pastries, cereal bars, frozen waffles and meat alternatives. The company's brands include Kellogg's®, Keebler®, Pop-Tarts®, Eggo®, Cheez-It®, Nutri-Grain®, Rice Krispies®, Murray®, Austin®, Morningstar Farms®, Famous Amos®, Carr's®, and Kashi®.

ADDRESS
One Kellogg Square
Battle Creek, MI 49016
www.kelloggcompany.com

KELLY SERVICES, INC.

VISION
To be the world's best staffing services company and to be recognized as the best.

MISSION
To serve our customers, employees, shareholders and society by providing a broad range of staffing services and products. To achieve our Mission:

We will develop innovative staffing services which meet the needs of our customers and contribute to their success.

We will foster an environment which stimulates professional excellence and encourages contribution by all employees.

We will provide our shareholders a fair return on their investment.

We will demonstrate good corporate citizenship through the ethical conduct of our business.

Note: Please refer to the company's website for its statements of Shared Values and Quality Policy.

CORPORATE DESCRIPTION
Kelly Services, Inc. is a *Fortune* 500 company headquartered in Troy, Michigan, offering staffing solutions that include temporary staffing services, staff leasing, outsourcing, vendor on-site, and full-time placement.

ADDRESS
999 West Big Beaver Road
Troy, MI 48084
www.kellyservices.com

LEVI STRAUSS & CO.

VALUES

Our values are fundamental to our success. They are the foundation of our company, define who we are and set us apart from the competition. They underlie our vision of the future, our business strategies and our decisions, actions and behaviors. We live by them. They endure.

Four core values are at the heart of Levi Strauss & Co.: Empathy, Originality, Integrity and Courage. These four values are linked. As we look at our history, we see a story of how our core values work together and are the source of our success.

Empathy — Walking in Other People's Shoes
Originality — Being Authentic and Innovative
Integrity — Doing the Right Thing
Courage — Standing Up for What We Believe

Note: For the full text that details each of the company's values above, as well as the company's vision statement, please refer to the company's website.

CORPORATE DESCRIPTION

Levi Strauss & Co. is one of the world's largest brand-name apparel marketers. The company manufactures and markets branded jeans and casual sportswear under the Levi's®, Dockers® and Levi Strauss Signature™ brands.

ADDRESS

1155 Battery Street
San Francisco, CA 94111
www.levistrauss.com

LILLY (ELI LILLY AND COMPANY)

THE LILLY DIFFERENCE—MISSION

We provide customers "Answers That Matter" through innovative medicines, information, and exceptional customer service that enable people to live longer, healthier, and more active lives.

STRATEGIC INTENT

By providing for the unmet needs of our customers through a continuous stream of innovation, we will outgrow all competitors.

VISION

"Answers That Matter" is the foundation of our promise to our customers. We will deliver on our promise by listening to and understanding the needs of our customers and providing unmatched value.

To provide our customers unmatched value, we will create four dimensions of competitive advantage:

• generating an accelerating flow of pharmaceutical products from internal discovery and external sources that address our customers' unmet needs

• manufacturing and supplying our portfolio of products at an ever-increasing level of quality and service

• providing information, services, and delivery systems that maximize the customer-defined value and that drive the early and sustained adoption of our products

• partnering to obtain access to high-potential molecules and strengthen key capabilities, thereby creating more value for Lilly and our partner from Lilly assets than we could achieve on our own

LILLY (ELI LILLY
AND COMPANY) (CONTINUED)

Our organization will be adaptive and highly flexible, allowing us to respond to both internal and external changes.

CORPORATE DESCRIPTION

Eli Lilly is a leading innovation-driven pharmaceutical company. The company employs more than 44,000 people worldwide and markets medicines in 143 countries.

ADDRESS

Lilly Corporate Center
Indianapolis, IN 46285
www.lilly.com

LOCKHEED MARTIN

VISION STATEMENT

To be the world's best advanced technology systems integrator.

MISSION/PURPOSE STATEMENT

To achieve Mission Success by attaining total customer satisfaction and meeting all our commitments.

Note: Please refer to the company's website to see its Values statement that accompanies the Vision and Mission/Purpose statements.

CORPORATE DESCRIPTION

Headquartered in Bethesda, Maryland, Lockheed Martin employs about 130,000 people worldwide and is principally engaged in the research, design, development, manufacture and integration of advanced technology systems, products, and services.

ADDRESS

6801 Rockledge Drive
Bethesda, MD 20817
www.lockheedmartin.com

MANPOWER INC.

VISION
Our Vision is to lead in the creation and delivery of services that enable our clients to win in the changing world of work.

Note: Please refer to the company's website for its Strategies and Values statements.

CORPORATE DESCRIPTION
Manpower Inc. (NYSE: MAN) is a world leader in the employment services industry; creating and delivering services that enable its clients to win in the changing world of work. Manpower offers employers a range of services for the entire employment and business cycle including permanent, temporary, and contract recruitment; employment assessment and selection; training; outplacement; outsourcing, and consulting.

ADDRESS
5301 North Ironwood Road
Milwaukee, WI 53217
www.manpower.com

MBIA INSURANCE CORPORATION

MBIA'S MISSION STATEMENT

As a world class manager of credit risk, we help our clients achieve their financial goals by providing Triple-A access to global capital markets and superior asset management services.

VALUES

Integrity—We embrace our Standard of Conduct by demonstrating principled behavior, honesty, and respect for everyone we work with each day. Promises made, promises kept.

Teamwork—We are committed to each other, bound by trust and loyalty. Our diversity makes us stronger; everyone's contribution matters. Our continuous personal development allows us to excel.

Performance Excellence—We are dedicated to our Foundation Principles through superb execution in everything we do. We act like owners, always seeking to exceed expectations, always acknowledging our fiduciary responsibilities.

FOUNDATION PRINCIPLES

Maintain the strongest team
No-loss underwriting
Triple-A ratings
Enhance long-term shareholder value

CORPORATE DESCRIPTION

MBIA Inc., through its subsidiaries, is a premier financial guarantor and provider of specialized financial products and services. The company's core business is credit enhancement of municipal bonds and asset- and mortgage-backed transactions in the new issue and secondary markets, internationally and domestically.

MBIA INSURANCE CORPORATION (CONTINUED)

ADDRESS
113 King Street
Armonk, NY 10504
www.mbia.com

MCKESSON CORPORATION

OUR MISSION
McKesson Corporation's mission is advancing the health of the health care system by advancing the success of our partners.

OUR VISION
Our strategic vision is to be healthcare's preferred provider of:

- pharmaceutical and medical supplies
- information solutions
- services and automation

CORPORATE DESCRIPTION
McKesson Corporation is the leading provider of supply, information, and care management products and services designed to reduce costs and improve quality across healthcare.

ADDRESS
One Post Street
San Francisco, CA 94104
www.mckesson.com

MEN'S WEARHOUSE

MISSION

The mission of Men's Wearhouse is to maximize sales, provide value to our customers and deliver top quality customer service while still having fun and maintaining our values.

These values include nurturing creativity, growing together, admitting to mistakes, promoting a happy and healthy lifestyle, enhancing a sense of community and striving toward becoming self-actualized people.

CORPORATE DESCRIPTION

The Men's Wearhouse, Inc. and its subsidiaries is a specialty retailer of menswear. They operate throughout the United States primarily under the brand names Men's Wearhouse and K&G and under the brand name of Moores in Canada.

ADDRESS

10485 West Bellfort Drive
Houston, TX 77031
www.menswearhouse.com

MERCK & CO., INC.

OUR MISSION

The mission of Merck is to provide society with superior products and services by developing innovations and solutions that improve the quality of life and satisfy customer needs, and to provide employees with meaningful work and advancement opportunities, and investors with a superior rate of return.

Note: Please refer to the company's website for its statement of Our Values.

CORPORATE DESCRIPTION

Merck & Co., Inc. is a global research-driven pharmaceutical company dedicated to putting patients first. Established in 1891, Merck discovers, develops, manufactures, and markets vaccines and medicines to address unmet medical needs.

ADDRESS

One Merck Drive
Whitehouse Station, NJ 08889
www.merck.com

MICROSOFT CORPORATION

OUR MISSION

At Microsoft, we work to help people and businesses throughout the world realize their full potential. This is our mission. Everything we do reflects this mission and the values that make it possible.

Note: Please refer to the company's website for its Values statement.

CORPORATE DESCRIPTION

Founded in 1975, Microsoft (NASDAQ: MSFT) is the worldwide leader in software, services and solutions that help people and businesses realize their full potential.

ADDRESS

One Microsoft Way
Redmond, WA 98052
www.microsoft.com

NALCO COMPANY

NALCO COMPANY MISSION STATEMENT

Our primary reason to exist is to create value for our customers by developing and implementing innovative, differentiated solutions that are financially, technically and environmentally sustainable.

NALCO'S VALUES

Our knowledge of our customers' industries and our technological expertise allow us to understand their current requirements and anticipate challenges. We uncover opportunities for enhancing our customers' processes and systems with innovative solutions that are financially, technically, and environmentally sustainable. Every day Nalco people deliver results that help our customers succeed by living our core values:

- Integrity
- Knowledge
- Initiative
- Communication
- Accountability

Nalco is people you trust, delivering results.

CORPORATE DESCRIPTION

Nalco Company is the leading provider of integrated water treatment and process improvement services, chemicals and equipment programs for industrial and institutional applications.

ADDRESS

1601 West Diehl Road
Naperville, IL 60563-1198
www.nalco.com

NATIONAL SEMICONDUCTOR CORPORATION

MISSION

National Semiconductor creates analog-intensive solutions that provide more energy efficiency, portability, better audio and sharper images in electronics systems.

CORPORATE DESCRIPTION

National Semiconductor, the industry's premier analog company, creates high performance analog devices and subsystems. National's leading-edge products include power management circuits, display drivers, audio and operational amplifiers, communication interface products and data conversion solutions.

ADDRESS

2900 Semiconductor Drive
Santa Clara, CA 95051
www.national.com

NEW YORK LIFE
INSURANCE COMPANY

OUR MISSION

Our mission is to provide financial security and peace of mind through our insurance, annuity and investment products and services.

By continuing to be a mutual company, we are uniquely aligned with our customers.

By maintaining superior financial strength, we protect their future.

By acting with integrity and humanity, we earn their trust and loyalty.

Every decision we make, every action we take, has one overriding purpose:

To be here when our customers need us.
That's why we call ourselves the company you keep.

CORPORATE DESCRIPTION

New York Life Insurance Company, a *Fortune* 100 company founded in 1845, is the largest mutual life insurance company in the United States and one of the largest life insurers in the world. Headquartered in New York City, New York Life's family of companies offers life insurance, annuities and long-term care insurance. New York Life Investment Management LLC provides institutional asset management and retirement plan services. Other New York Life affiliates provide an array of securities products and services, as well as institutional and retail mutual funds.

ADDRESS

51 Madison Avenue
New York, NY 10010
www.newyorklife.com

NIKE, INC.

MISSION
To bring inspiration and innovation to every athlete in the world.

"If you have a body, you are an athlete."—Bill Bowerman

CORPORATE DESCRIPTION
NIKE's principal business activity is the design, development, distribution, and worldwide marketing of high quality footwear, apparel, equipment, and accessory products. NIKE is the largest seller of branded athletic footwear and apparel in the world.

ADDRESS
One Bowerman Drive
Beaverton, OR 97005-6453
www.nike.com

NORFOLK SOUTHERN CORPORATION

VISION

Be the safest, most customer-focused and successful transportation company in the world.

MISSION

Norfolk Southern's mission is to enhance the value of our stockholders' investment over time by providing quality freight transportation services and undertaking any other related businesses in which our resources, particularly our people, give the company an advantage.

Note: Please refer to the company's website for its Creed statement.

CORPORATE DESCRIPTION

Norfolk Southern Corporation is a Norfolk, Virginia-based company that controls a major freight railroad, Norfolk Southern Railway Company. The railway operates approximately 21,300 route miles in twenty-two eastern states, the District of Columbia and Ontario, Canada; serves all major eastern ports; and connects with rail partners in the West and Canada, linking customers to markets around the world. Norfolk Southern provides comprehensive logistics services and offers the most extensive intermodal network in the East.

ADDRESS

Three Commercial Place
Norfolk, VA 23510
www.nscorp.com

NORTHWESTERN MUTUAL

THE NORTHWESTERN MUTUAL WAY

The ambition of The Northwestern has been less to be large than to be safe; its aim is to rank first in benefits to policyowners rather than first in size. Valuing quality above quantity, it has preferred to secure its business under certain salutary restrictions and limitations rather than to write a much larger business at the possible sacrifice of those valuable points that have made The Northwestern pre-eminently the policyholder's Company. —Executive Committee, 1888

CORPORATE DESCRIPTION

Northwestern Mutual offers life insurance, disability income, annuities, long-term care insurance, and investment products and services that help provide for a lifetime of financial security.

ADDRESS

720 East Wisconsin Avenue
Milwaukee, WI 53202
www.nmfn.com

OCCIDENTAL PETROLEUM CORPORATION

OUR VISION

Clean, efficient and reliable energy supplies are critical to the growth and development of the global economy. In the United States and other industrialized nations, energy is often taken for granted, but cheap, reliable energy is what fuels economic vitality and makes possible our high-tech world, our modern lifestyles and our convenient transportation options. In developing nations, energy is a critical driver of sustained economic expansion that brings more jobs, better health care, improved educational opportunities, and higher living standards overall. As the world's demands grow, so does the need for additional energy resources.

Occidental Petroleum Corporation has the expertise and experience to find and develop new sources of oil and natural gas today to fuel tomorrow's economic growth—without compromising our strong commitment to protecting the environment, promoting our high standards of social responsibility and safeguarding the health and safety of employees and neighbors.

CORPORATE DESCRIPTION

Occidental Petroleum Corporation (NYSE: OXY) is a world leader in oil and natural gas exploration and production and a major North American chemical manufacturer.

ADDRESS

10889 Wilshire Boulevard
Los Angeles, CA 90024
www.oxy.com

PEPSICO

OUR MISSION

We aspire to make PepsiCo the world's premier consumer products company, focused on convenient foods and beverages. We seek to produce healthy financial rewards for investors as we provide opportunities for growth and enrichment to our employees, our business partners, and the communities in which we operate. And in everything we do, we strive to act with honesty, openness, fairness, and integrity.

CORPORATE DESCRIPTION

PepsiCo is a leading, global snack and beverage company. Its principle businesses include Frito-Lay snacks, Pepsi-Cola beverages, Gatorade sports drinks, Quaker foods, and Tropicana juices.

ADDRESS

700 Anderson Hill Road
Purchase, NY 10577
www.pepsico.com

THE PROGRESSIVE GROUP OF INSURANCE COMPANIES

OUR VALUES

Progressive's vision is to reduce the human trauma and economic costs associated with automobile accidents. We do this by providing our customers with services designed to help them get their lives back in order again as quickly as possible.

Governing our vision, decisions and behavior are our core values—pragmatic statements of what works best for us in the real world.

Integrity. We revere honesty. We adhere to the highest ethical standards, provide timely, accurate, and complete financial reporting, encourage disclosing bad news; and welcome disagreement.

Golden Rule. We respect all people, value the differences among them, and deal with them in the way we want to be dealt with. This requires us to know ourselves and to try to understand others.

Objectives. We strive to communicate clearly Progressive's ambitious objectives and our people's personal and team objectives. We evaluate performance against all these objectives.

Excellence. We strive constantly to improve in order to meet and exceed the highest expectations of our customers, shareholders and people. We teach and encourage our people to improve performance and to reduce the costs of what they do for customers. We base their rewards on results and promotion on ability.

Profit. The opportunity to earn a profit is how the competitive free-enterprise system motivates investment to enhance human health and happiness. Expanding profits reflect our customers' and claimants' increasingly positive view of Progressive.

THE PROGRESSIVE GROUP
OF INSURANCE COMPANIES (CONTINUED)

CORPORATE DESCRIPTION

The Progressive Group of Insurance Companies, in business since 1937, ranks third in the nation for auto insurance, based on premiums written, and provides drivers with competitive rates and 24/7, in-person and on-line service. The products and services of the Progressive Direct Group of Insurance Companies are marketed directly to consumers through the Progressive Direct℠ brand and by phone at 1-800-PROGRESSIVE and online at progressivedirect.com.

ADDRESS

6300 Wilson Mills Road
Mayfield Village, OH 44143
www.progressive.com

PUBLIX SUPER MARKETS, INC.

OUR MISSION

Our mission at Publix is to be the **premier quality food retailer in the world.** To that end we commit to be:

- Passionately focused on **Customer Value,**
- **Intolerant** of **Waste,**
- **Dedicated** to the **Dignity, Value,** and **Employment Security** of our **Associates,**
- **Devoted** to the highest standards of **Stewardship** for our **Stockholders,** and
- **Involved** as **Responsible Citizens** in our **Communities.**

CORPORATE DESCRIPTION

Founded in 1930, Publix Super Markets is the largest and fastest-growing employee-owned supermarket chain in the United States.

ADDRESS

P.O. Box 407
Lakeland, FL 33802
www.publix.com

QWEST COMMUNICATIONS

QWEST VISION

Qwest is the premier provider of full-service communications for people at work, at home, or on the move. Qwest's competency reaches across America, drawing on the Spirit of Service at the heart of our heritage as we effectively steward our shareowners' investments and provide outstanding service to the customers we serve. As our dedicated professionals move and manage information, we do so ethically and with integrity, providing superior value and advanced products and services, assuming only those tasks we can do exceedingly well.

Note: Please refer to the company's website for its Values and Ethics statement.

CORPORATE DESCRIPTION

Qwest Communications International, Inc. (NYSE: Q) is a leading provider of voice, video and data services. The company's approximately 40,000 employees are committed to the "Spirit of Service" and to providing world-class services that exceed customers' expectations for quality, value, and reliability.

ADDRESS

1801 California Street
Denver, CO 80202
www.qwest.com

RADIOSHACK CORPORATION

VISION (WHAT WE WANT TO BE)
RadioShack is guided by its vision to be the most powerful one-stop shop to connect people with the wonders of modern technology.

MISSION (WHY WE EXIST)
RadioShack's mission is to demystify technology in every neighborhood in America.

VALUES (WHAT'S IMPORTANT TO US)
Teamwork:
- We are the company; there is no "they"
- We work together for common objectives
- We consider the effect of action on others
- We all work for our customers

Pride:
- Commitment to excellence
- Self-respect
- Believing in and promoting the value of our company, associates, and products
- Dedication to competitive achievement

Trust:
- Share the truth, both good and bad
- Placing confidence in others to perform
- Empowering people to do their best

Integrity:
- Doing the right thing, even when no one is watching
- Honesty and openness in relationships with associates, customers, shareholders, and vendors
- Fair and equal access to opportunity

RADIOSHACK CORPORATION (CONTINUED)

STRATEGY (OUR GAME PLAN FOR SUCCESS)

Under our brand position—"You've Got Questions. We've Got Answers."—RadioShack is focused on a solutions strategy: To dominate cost-effective solutions to meet everyone's routine electronics needs and families' distinct electronics wants. This means creating a shopping experience that is convenient, contemporary and fun, and for our knowledgeable sales associates to forge personal relationships with our customers based on honesty, trust, helpfulness and an understanding of individual wants and needs.

CORPORATE DESCRIPTION

Fort Worth, Texas-based RadioShack Corporation (NYSE: RSH) is the nation's most trusted consumer electronics specialty retailer and a growing provider of business-to-business retail support services.

ADDRESS

300 RadioShack Circle
Fort Worth, TX 76102
www.radioshackcorporation.com

RAYTHEON AIRCRAFT COMPANY

VISION

To be recognized as the world's leading general aviation manufacturer, always making product quality and customer service our highest priorities.

Note: Please refer to the company's website for its Strategy, Goals and Values statements.

CORPORATE DESCRIPTION

Raytheon Aircraft Company is the world's leading business and special-mission aircraft manufacturer, providing a wide variety of aviation products and services for businesses, governments, and individuals.

ADDRESS

15011 East Central
Wichita, KS 67201
www.raytheonaircraft.com

RICH PRODUCTS
CORPORATION

THE RICH FAMILY VISION—A LONG-TERM COMMITMENT
We will excel as an innovative family-owned company who treats our customers like family. We will be their first choice as a long-term business partner because we are reliable, responsive to their needs, easy-to-do business with, and committed to providing great-tasting, quality products and customized solutions to help them grow their business.

THE RICH MISSION
The Rich Mission strives to set new standards of excellence in customer satisfaction and to achieve new levels of competitive success in every category of business in which we operate. We will achieve this by working together as a team to:

Impress Our Customers. Provide exceptional service to our external and internal customers the first time and every time.

Improve, Improve, Improve! Continuously improve the quality and value of the goods we produce and services we provide.

Empower People. Unleash the talents of all our Associates by creating an environment that is safe, that recognizes and rewards their achievements, and encourages their participation and growth.

Work Smarter. Drive out all waste of time, effort and material—all the barriers and extra steps that keep us from doing our jobs right.

Do the Right Thing! Maintain the highest standards of integrity and ethical conduct and behave as good citizens in our communities.

Think Outside the Box. Challenge the status quo and look for opportunities to make breakthrough innovations in Products, Processes, and Services.

CORPORATE DESCRIPTION

Rich Products Corporation is known around the world as the founder of the nondairy segment of the frozen food industry and a leading supplier and solutions provider to the food service, in-store bakery, and retail marketplaces. One of the world's premier family-owned food companies, Rich's posts annual sales exceeding $2 billion.

ADDRESS

One Robert Rich Way
Buffalo, NY 14213
www.richs.com

SARA LEE CORPORATION

OUR MISSION
To simply delight you…every day.

OUR VISION
To be the first choice of consumers and customers around the world by bringing together innovative ideas, continuous process improvement and people who make things happen.

Note: Please refer to the company's website for its statement of Our Values.

CORPORATE DESCRIPTION
Sara Lee Corporation is a Chicago-based global manufacturer and marketer of high-quality, brand-name products for consumers throughout the world. In February 2005, the company began executing a bold and ambitious multi-year plan to transform Sara Lee into a company focused on food, beverage, and household and body care businesses around the world. As part of its transformation plan, Sara Lee will drive growth in its key categories via strong brands such as Ball Park, Douwe Egberts, Hillshire Farm, Jimmy Dean, Kiwi, Sanex, Senseo and its namesake, Sara Lee.

ADDRESS
Three First National Plaza
70 West Madison Street
Chicago, IL 60602
www.saralee.com

SCHERING-PLOUGH CORPORATION

VISION: TO EARN TRUST, EVERY DAY.

We aspire to earn the trust of doctors, patients and customers as a champion for them and as a company that provides them with a steady flow of innovative, science-based medicines and services. By earning trust, we will build growth.

MISSION

To work to become:

1. The innovation, quality, and service leader among our primary care and specialty customers and patients, and the best "customer-touch" company in our industry, as judged by our customers.

2. The most effective company in our industry at managing product flow.

3. The best-managed company as defined by functional competencies, alignment around goals and behaviors, business integrity, teamwork, productivity and cost-consciousness.

4. The most improved company in our industry and, ultimately, the company in our industry that is most trusted by key stakeholders.

5. Known for our leadership edge achieved by our passion for excellence.

Note: Please refer to the company's website for its Leader Behaviors and Values statements.

CORPORATE DESCRIPTION

Schering-Plough is a global, science-based health care company with leading prescription, consumer and animal health products. Through internal research and collaborations with partners, Schering-Plough

SCHERING-PLOUGH
CORPORATION (CONTINUED)

discovers, develops, manufactures, and markets advanced drug thera-
pies to meet important medical needs. Schering-Plough's vision is to
earn the trust of the physicians, patients, and customers served by its
more than 30,000 people around the world.

ADDRESS
2000 Galloping Hill Road
Kenilworth, NJ 07033
www.sgp.com or www.schering-plough.com

SCHWAB (THE CHARLES SCHWAB CORPORATION)

CHARLES SCHWAB MISSION & VALUES

Our mission is to provide the most useful and ethical financial services in the world.

Our Core Values are to:

- Be fair, empathetic and responsive in serving our clients
- Respect and reinforce our fellow employees and the power of team-work
- Strive relentlessly to innovate what we do and how we do it
- Always earn and be worthy of our client's trust

CORPORATE DESCRIPTION

The Charles Schwab Corporation (NASDAQ: SCHW), through its operating subsidiaries, provides securities brokerage and financial services to individual investors and the independent investment advisors who work with them. With over 7 million individual investor accounts and more than $1 trillion in client assets, The Charles Schwab Corporation is one of the nation's largest financial services firms.

ADDRESS

101 Montgomery Street
San Francisco, CA 94104
www.schwab.com

SCRIPPS
(THE E.W. SCRIPPS COMPANY)

STATEMENT OF PURPOSE

The E.W. Scripps Company strives for excellence in the products and services we produce and responsible service to the communities in which we operate. Our purpose is to continue to engage in successful, growing enterprises in the fields of information and entertainment. The company intends to expand, develop, and acquire new products and services, and to pursue new market opportunities. Our focus shall be long-term growth for the benefit of shareholders and employees.

CORPORATE DESCRIPTION

Scripps is a diverse media concern with interests in national lifestyle television networks, newspaper publishing, broadcast television, television retailing, interactive media and licensing and syndication. All of the company's media businesses provide content and advertising services via the Internet.

ADDRESS

312 Walnut Street
Cincinnati, OH 45202
www.scripps.com

SMUCKER'S
(THE J.M. SMUCKER COMPANY)

VISION STATEMENT

We will own and market food brands which hold the #1 market position in their respective category, with an emphasis on North America.

We will achieve balanced growth through:

- Increased market share of our brands
- Acquisition of other leading food brands
- New products that provide convenience, are good and "good for you," and make the consumer smile

CORPORATE DESCRIPTION

The J.M. Smucker Company was founded in 1897 when the Company's namesake and founder sold his first product—apple butter—from the back of a horse-drawn wagon. Today, over a century later, the Company is the market leader in fruit spreads, peanut butter, shortening and oils, ice cream toppings, and health foods and natural beverages in North America under such icon brands as Smucker's®, Jif® and Crisco®. The family of brands also includes Pillsbury® baking mixes and ready-to-spread frostings; Hungry Jack® pancake mixes, syrups and potato side dishes; and Martha White® baking mixes and ingredients in the U.S.; along with Robin Hood® flour and baking mixes, and Bick's® pickles and condiments in Canada.

ADDRESS

One Strawberry Lane
Orrville, OH 44667
www.smuckers.com

SONOCO

STRATEGIC MISSION STATEMENT

Sonoco intends to be the low-cost global leader in providing customer-preferred packaging solutions to selected value-added segments, where we expect to be either number one or two in market share. Shareholder return, customer and employee satisfaction, and commitment to excellence, integrity, environmental stewardship and a safe workplace will be the hallmarks of our culture.

Note: Please refer to the company's website for its Strategic Objectives and People, Culture and Values statements.

CORPORATE DESCRIPTION

Founded in 1899, Sonoco (NYSE: SON) is a $3.5 billion global manufacturer of industrial and consumer products and provider of packaging services, with more than 300 operations in thirty-five countries, serving customers in some eighty-five nations.

ADDRESS

1 North Second Street
Hartsville, SC 29550
www.sonoco.com

SOUTHWEST AIRLINES

THE MISSION OF SOUTHWEST AIRLINES
The mission of Southwest Airlines is dedication to the highest quality of Customer Service delivered with a sense of warmth, friendliness, individual pride, and Company Spirit.

TO OUR EMPLOYEES
We are committed to provide our Employees a stable work environment with equal opportunities for learning and personal growth. Creativity and innovation are encouraged for improving the effectiveness of Southwest Airlines. Above all, employees will be provided the same concern, respect, and caring attitude within the organization that they are expected to share externally with every Southwest Customer.

CORPORATE DESCRIPTION
Southwest Airlines (NYSE: LUV) is a major domestic airline that provides primarily shorthaul, high-frequency, point-to-point, low-fare service. Today Southwest operates more than 400 Boeing 737 aircraft in sixty-two cities.

ADDRESS
P.O. Box 36611
Dallas, TX 75235
www.southwest.com

SPACELABS MEDICAL, INC.

VISION

Our vision is to be a globally active, progressive, and growing force in patient care solutions. We achieve this vision by delivering; innovative care solutions that improve outcomes and clinical efficiencies, and solutions that give care teams in hospitals throughout the world more time to care.

CORPORATE DESCRIPTION

Spacelabs Medical, Inc. is a global manufacturer and distributor of patient monitoring systems for critical care and anesthesia, wired and wireless networks and clinical information connectivity solutions, ambulatory blood pressure (AMP) monitors and medical data services. Spacelabs Medical is a division of Spacelabs Healthcare, Inc.

ADDRESS

P.O. Box 7018
Issaquah, WA 98927
www.spacelabs.com

STARWOOD HOTELS & RESORTS WORLDWIDE, INC.

COMPANY VALUES

Our values serve as the guide for how we treat our customers, our owners, our shareholders and our associates. We aspire to these values to make Starwood a great place to work and do business.

We succeed only when we meet and
exceed the expectations of our customers,
owners, and shareholders. We have a **passion for
excellence** and will deliver the highest
standards of **integrity** and **fairness**. We celebrate
the **diversity** of people, ideas, and cultures.
We honor the **dignity** and **value of
individuals** working as a team. We improve the
communities in which we work.
We encourage **innovation,** accept
accountability, and embrace **change.**
We seek knowledge and growth through **learning.**
We share a **sense of urgency, nimbleness,**
and endeavor **to have fun,** too.

STARWOOD'S MISSION:

To our Shareholders: Our goal is to grow EBITDA at least 8%–10% per year and EPS at least 15% per year.

To our Customers: We want Starwood to be the easiest company with which to do business.

And to our Employees: Our commitment is to make Starwood a great place to work.

STARWOOD HOTELS & RESORTS WORLDWIDE, INC. (CONTINUED)

CORPORATE DESCRIPTION

Starwood Hotels & Resorts Worldwide, Inc. is one of the leading hotel and leisure companies in the world with approximately 750 properties in more than eighty countries and 120,000 employees at its owned and managed properties. With internationally renowned brands, Starwood® corporation is a fully integrated owner, operator and franchisor of hotels and resorts including: St. Regis®, The Luxury Collection®, Sheraton®, Westin®, Four Points® by Sheraton, and W® Hotels and Resorts as well as Starwood Vacation Ownership, Inc., one of the premier developers and operators of high quality vacation interval ownership resorts.

ADDRESS

1111 Westchester Avenue
White Plains, NY 10604
www.starwoodhotels.com

STEELCASE INC.

MISSION
To provide a better work experience.

VISION
To understand the needs of users, facility managers, architects and designers and dealers better than anyone else.

CORPORATE DESCRIPTION
Steelcase, the global leader in the office furniture industry, helps people have a better work experience by providing products, services and insights into the ways people work. The company designs and manufactures architecture, furniture and technology products. Founded in 1912 and headquartered in Grand Rapids, Michigan, Steelcase (NYSE: SCS) serves customers through a network of more than 800 independent dealers and approximately 14,000 employees worldwide.

ADDRESS
901 44th Street SE
Grand Rapids, MI 49508
www.steelcase.com

SUNOCO, INC.

OUR PURPOSE

To be a source of excellence for our customers; to provide a challenging professional experience for our employees; to be a rewarding investment for our shareholders; to be a respected citizen of community and country.

CORPORATE DESCRIPTION

Sunoco, Inc. (NYSE: SUN), headquartered in Philadelphia, Pennsylvania, is a leading manufacturer and marketer of petroleum and petrochemical products. With 900,000 barrels per day of refining capacity, approximately 4,800 retail sites selling gasoline and convenience items, approximately 4,500 miles of Sunoco-owned and operated crude oil and refined product pipelines and thirty-eight product terminals, Sunoco is one of the largest independent refiner-marketers in the United States. Sunoco is a significant manufacturer of petrochemicals with annual sales of approximately 5 billion pounds, largely chemical intermediates used to make fibers, plastics, film, and resins. Utilizing a unique, patented technology, Sunoco also has the capacity to manufacture over 2.5 million tons annually of high-quality, metallurgical-grade coke for use in the steel industry.

ADDRESS

1735 Market Street
Philadelphia, PA 19103
www.sunocoinc.com

SYSCO CORPORATION

MISSION STATEMENT
Helping our customers succeed

CORPORATE DESCRIPTION
SYSCO, the largest foodservice marketing and distribution organization in North America, provides food and related products and services to approximately 400,000 restaurants, healthcare and educational facilities, lodging establishments, and other foodservice customers, generating sales of approximately $30 billion for calendar year 2004. SYSCO's operations, supported by approximately 46,000 associates, are located throughout the United States and Canada and include broadline foodservice distribution companies, specialty produce and custom-cut meat operations, Asian cuisine foodservice distributors, hotel supply operations, and chain restaurant distribution subsidiaries.

ADDRESS
1390 Enclave Parkway
Houston, TX 77077
www.sysco.com

TENET HEALTHCARE CORPORATION

MISSION AND VALUES
Tenet's name and logo reflect its core business philosophy—the importance of shared values between partners in providing a full spectrum of quality, cost-efficient health care.

OUR VISION
Tenet will distinguish itself as a leader in redefining health care delivery and will be recognized for the passion of its people and partners in providing quality, innovative care to the patients it serves in each community.

OUR TENETS
Successful partnerships require that the parties share certain beliefs, that they hold philosophies, expectations and standards in common. Tenet has articulated our beliefs in a list of Our Tenets.

Note: Please refer to the company's website for a link to Our Tenets statement.

COMPACT WITH COMMUNITIES
Tenet recognizes our vital responsibilities as a member of the community.

Note: Please refer to the company's website to learn more about Compact with Communities.

COMPACT WITH UNINSURED PATIENTS
Tenet has taken a leadership position in proposing solutions for the problem of the uninsured.

Note: Please refer to the company's website to learn more about Compact with Uninsured Patients.

CORPORATE DESCRIPTION

Tenet Healthcare Corporation, through its subsidiaries, owns and operates acute care hospitals and related health care services. Tenet's hospitals aim to provide the best possible care to every patient who comes through their doors, with a clear focus on quality and service.

ADDRESS

13737 Noel Road
Dallas, TX 75240
www.tenethealth.com

TEXAS INSTRUMENTS

TI VISION STATEMENT
World leadership in digital solutions for the networked society.

TI VALUES
Integrity
Innovation
Commitment

TI PRINCIPLES
We respect and value people.
We are honest.
We learn and create.
We act boldly.
We take responsibility.
We commit to win.

CORPORATE DESCRIPTION
Texas Instruments Incorporated (NYSE: TXN) provides innovative DSP and analog technologies to meet our customers' real world signal processing requirements. In addition to Semiconductor, the company's businesses include Sensors & Controls and Educational & Productivity Solutions. TI is headquartered in Dallas, Texas, and has manufacturing, design, or sales operations in more than twenty-five countries.

ADDRESS
12500 TI Boulevard
Dallas, TX 75243
www.ti.com

THOR INDUSTRIES, INC.

MISSION

Thor will continue to be the best recreation vehicle and bus company in North America.

CORPORATE DESCRIPTION

Thor Industries, Inc., founded in 1980, is the world's largest manufacturer of recreation vehicles which account for 90% of sales and is a major manufacturer of commercial buses (10% of sales). Sales are approximately $3 billion. Thor has a 31% market share of the towable RV market, 13% of the motorized RV market, and 43% of the small and mid-size commercial bus market. Thor's market capitalization of approximately $2.5 billion is about as large as the five other public RV manufacturers combined.

ADDRESS

419 West Pike Street
P.O. Box 629
Jackson Center, OH 45334
www.thorindustries.com

TIFFANY & CO.

MISSION STATEMENT

Tiffany & Co. seeks to enrich the lives of its customers by creating enduring objects of extraordinary beauty that will be cherished for generations.

Our mission is to be recognized as the world's most respected and successful designer, manufacturer and marketer of the finest jewelry, timepieces, selected accessories and tabletop products. Success in achieving our overall mission is defined in terms of specific product, service and stakeholder missions.

Our product mission is to produce objects of timeless design using the purest materials and exhibiting the finest craftsmanship. Our products represent the world of good taste. Tiffany products do not go out of style and remain above the whim of fashion. They offer our customers lasting value and hold their beauty and excitement from one generation to the next.

Our service mission is to be recognized for the warmth, graciousness, and efficiency of our sales and service professionals. We will engage our customers in consultative dialogue, share our expert knowledge, and build enduring relationships with them. We will unfailingly honor our commitments.

Our stakeholder mission reflects our commitments to our employees, our shareholders, and the communities that sustain us. For our employees, we will create an environment that recognizes and rewards creativity, initiative, and dedication and respects diversity, dignity and the shared values of community and family. We will respect the laws, customs, and values of our host communities and work to enrich those communities through the participation of our employees in civil society and through our financial support of community aspirations. For our shareholders, we will seek to generate superior financial returns with business, accounting and ethical practices that exhibit integrity and transparency.

CORPORATE DESCRIPTION

Tiffany & Co. is a holding company that operates through its subsidiary companies. The Company's principal subsidiary, Tiffany and Company, is a jeweler and specialty retailer, whose merchandise offerings include an extensive selection of fine jewelry (82% of net sales in fiscal year 2004), as well as timepieces, sterling silverware, china, crystal, stationery, fragrances and accessories. Through Tiffany and Company and other subsidiaries, the Company is engaged in product design, manufacturing and retailing activities.

ADDRESS

727 Fifth Avenue
New York, NY 10022
www.tiffany.com

TOOTSIE ROLL INDUSTRIES, INC.

CORPORATE PRINCIPLES

We believe that the differences among companies are attributable to the caliber of their people, and therefore we strive to attract and retain superior people for each job.

We believe that an open family atmosphere at work combined with professional management fosters cooperation and enables each individual to maximize his or her contribution to the company and realize the corresponding rewards.

We do not jeopardize long-term growth for immediate, short-term results.

We maintain a conservative financial posture in the deployment and management of our assets.

We run a trim operation and continually strive to eliminate waste, minimize cost and implement performance improvements.

We invest in the latest and most productive equipment to deliver the best quality product to our customers at the lowest cost.

We seek to outsource functions where appropriate and to vertically integrate operations where it is financially advantageous to do so.

We view our well known brands as prized assets to be aggressively advertised and promoted to each new generation of consumers.

We conduct business with the highest ethical standards and integrity which are codified in the Company's "Code of Business Conduct and Ethics."

CORPORATE DESCRIPTION

Tootsie Roll Industries, Inc. has been engaged in the manufacture and sale of confectionery products for 108 years. Our products are primarily sold under the familiar brand names Tootsie Roll, Tootsie Roll Pops, Caramel Apple Pops, Child's Play, Charms, Blow Pop, Blue Razz, Cella's chocolate covered cherries, Mason Dots, Mason Crows, Junior Mints, Charleston Chew, Sugar Daddy, Sugar Babies, Andes, Fluffy Stuff cotton candy, Dubble Bubble, Razzles, Cry Baby, Nik-L-Nip, and El Bubble.

ADDRESS

7401 South Cicero Avenue
Chicago, IL 60629
www.tootsie.com

TRACTOR SUPPLY COMPANY

MISSION

To work hard, have fun, and make money by providing legendary service and great products at everyday low prices.

Our Business: We are committed to be the most dependable supplier of basic maintenance products to farm, ranch, and rural customers.

Our People: We value honesty, integrity, mutual respect, and teamwork above all else.

We are an open company where everyone has the information and tools to grow and excel.

We encourage risk taking, celebrate initiative, and reward success.

Our Stakeholders: We are a growth company. We consistently grow sales and profits by continuous improvement throughout the company.

Note: Please refer to the company's website for its Values statement.

CORPORATE DESCRIPTION

Tractor Supply Company (NASDAQ: TSCO) is the largest retail farm and ranch store chain in the United States. The company operates more than 550 retail stores in thirty-four states, employs more than 7,800 team members and is headquartered in Brentwood, Tennessee.

ADDRESS

200 Powell Place
Brentwood, TN 37027
www.mytscstore.com

VALASSIS

PLEDGE TO SHAREHOLDERS
As employees and fellow "owners" of the company, we are committed to achieving maximum profits, long-term growth, and a fair return on your investment. We realize that, next to our clients, our shareholders are the key to our success. Therefore, we promise to manage your investment by working diligently to achieve our long-term growth plan. We will constantly look for ways to improve and expand our products and services, set and accomplish challenging objectives for ourselves and for our company, increase efficiencies through training and innovation, and conduct our business ethically and responsibly.

VISION
Valassis will be an innovative, integrated marketing solutions company focused on customers in a broad range of industries.

VALUES
People: We believe that our people are our most important resource.
Passion: We have a passion for success.
Responsibility: We share the responsibility for making this a great company.
Integrity: We value integrity and mutual trust.
Innovation: We encourage innovation.

CORPORATE DESCRIPTION
Valassis (NYSE: VCI) is a billion-dollar marketing services company that is publicly traded. It is the only company that provides a combination of home-delivered invited media products and services at the market, neighborhood, and household targeted levels and can integrate all three levels of targeting into a single solution.

VALASSIS (CONTINUED)

ADDRESS
19975 Victor Parkway
Livonia, MI 48152
www.valassis.com

VULCAN MATERIALS COMPANY

MISSION

Vulcan Materials Company is an international producer of industrial materials and commodities that are essential to the standard of living of advanced and developing societies.

Our Mission is to provide quality products and services which consistently meet our customers' expectations; to be responsible stewards with respect to the safety and environmental impact of our operations and products; and to earn superior returns for our shareholders.

We recognize that success in all of our activities is related directly to the talents, dedication and performance of our employees throughout the company.

Note: Please refer to the company's website for its Guiding Principles and Commitments statements.

CORPORATE DESCRIPTION

Vulcan Materials Company provides infrastructure materials that are required by the American economy. We are the nation's largest producer of construction aggregates and a leader in the production of other construction materials.

ADDRESS

1200 Urban Center Drive
P.O. Box 385014
Birmingham, AL 35242
www.vulcanmaterials.com

WELLS FARGO & COMPANY

VISION

We want to satisfy all of our customers' financial needs, help them succeed financially, be the premier provider of financial services in every one of our markets, and be known as one of America's great companies.

CORPORATE DESCRIPTION

Wells Fargo (NYSE: WFC) is a diversified financial services company—providing banking, insurance, investments, mortgage, and consumer finance—for more than 23 million customers through 6,200 stores, the Internet and other distribution channels across North America and internationally.

ADDRESS

420 Montgomery Street
San Francisco, CA 94104
www.wellsfargo.com

Please note: Materials concerning Wells Fargo are used with permission from Wells Fargo & Company.

WENDY'S INTERNATIONAL, INC.

MISSION

Our Mission is to deliver superior quality products and services for our customers and communities through leadership, innovation, and partnerships.

VISION

Our Vision is to be the quality leader in everything we do.

Note: Please refer to the company's website for its description of Core Values.

CORPORATE DESCRIPTION

Wendy's International, Inc. is one of the world's most successful restaurant operating and franchising companies, with more than 6,300 Wendy's Old Fashioned Hamburgers restaurants in North America and more than 300 international restaurants.

ADDRESS

One Dave Thomas Boulevard
Dublin, OH 43017
www.wendys.com

WINNEBAGO INDUSTRIES, INC.

MISSION STATEMENT

Winnebago Industries, Inc. is the leading United States manufacturer of motor homes and related products and services. Our mission is to continually improve our products and services to meet or exceed the expectations of our customers. We emphasize employee teamwork and involvement in identifying and implementing programs to save time and lower production costs while maintaining the highest quality of products. These strategies allow us to prosper as a business with a high degree of integrity and to provide a reasonable return for our shareholders, the ultimate owners of our business.

Note: Please refer to the company's website for its Values and Guiding Principles statements.

COMPANY PROFILE

Winnebago Industries, Inc., headquartered in Forest City, Iowa, is the leading United States manufacturer of motor homes and self-contained recreation vehicles used primarily in leisure travel and outdoor recreation activities.

ADDRESS

P.O. Box 152
Forest City, IA 50436
www.winnebagoind.com

WYETH

MISSION
We bring to the world pharmaceutical and health care products that improve lives and deliver outstanding value to our customers and shareholders.

VISION
Our vision is to lead the way to a healthier world. By carrying out this vision at every level of our organization, we will be recognized by our employees, customers, and shareholders as the best pharmaceutical company in the world, resulting in value for all.

We will achieve this by being accountable for:

- Leading the world in innovation through pharmaceutical, biotech, and vaccine technologies
- Making trust, quality, integrity, and excellence hallmarks of the way we do business
- Attracting, developing, and motivating our people
- Continually growing and improving our business
- Demonstrating efficiency in how we use resources and make decisions

Note: Please refer to the company's website for its Values statement.

CORPORATE DESCRIPTION
Wyeth is one of the world's largest research-driven pharmaceutical and health care products companies. It is a leader in the discovery, development, manufacturing, and marketing of pharmaceuticals, vaccines, biotechnology products, and nonprescription medicines that improve the quality of life for people worldwide. The company's major divisions include Wyeth Pharmaceuticals, Wyeth Consumer Healthcare, and Fort Dodge Animal Health.

WYETH

ADDRESS
5 Giralda Farms
Madison, NJ 07940
www.wyeth.com

XEROX CORPORATION

XEROX MISSION STATEMENT

Our strategic intent is to help people find better ways to do great work—
by constantly leading in document technologies, products, and services
that improve our customers' work processes and business results.

XEROX VALUES

Since our inception, we have operated under the guidance of six core
values:

We succeed through satisfied customers.
We deliver quality and excellence in all we do.
We require premium return on assets.
We use technology to develop market leadership.
We value and empower our employees.
We behave responsibly as a corporate citizen.

CORPORATE DESCRIPTION

Xerox Corporation is a technology and services enterprise that helps businesses deploy smarter document management strategies and find better
ways to work. It offers an array of innovative document solutions, services, and systems—including color and black-and-white printers, digital
presses, multifunction devices, and digital copiers—designed for offices
and production-printing environments. It also offers associated supplies,
software and support.

ADDRESS

800 Long Ridge Road
Stamford, CT 06904
www.xerox.com

ZALE CORPORATION

MISSION STATEMENT

The mission of Zale Corporation is to be the best fine jewelry retailer in North America. Our goal is to develop and market the finest collection of jewelry brands by creating a customer experience that builds lasting relationships and generates superior returns for our shareholders. To achieve this objective, we are committed to educate, motivate, and reward our employees to maximize the talents of each individual.

CORPORATE DESCRIPTION

Zale Corporation is North America's largest specialty retailer of fine jewelry operating approximately 2,350 retail locations throughout the United States, Canada, and Puerto Rico, as well as online. Zale Corporation's brands include Zales Jewelers, Zales Outlet, Gordon's Jewelers, Bailey Banks & Biddle, Peoples Jewellers, Mappins Jewellers, and Piercing Pagoda. Through its ZLC Direct organization, Zale also operates online at www.zales.com and www.baileybanksandbiddle.com.

ADDRESS

901 West Walnut Hill Lane
Irving, TX 75038
www.zalecorp.com

ABOUT THE AUTHOR

Jeffrey Abrahams is a graduate of the University of Iowa Writers' Workshop and a former journalist. He has been an award-winning advertising and marketing copywriter for small businesses and *Fortune* 500 companies for more than thirty years. His passion is to help people articulate and communicate their ideas, ideals, and goals. He lives in Oakland, California.